In Praise of
How to Enjoy Your Retirement

"There can be no such thing as one simple retirement plan that will be best for all. What the authors of this wise and entertaining work have done is save the rest of us a good deal of study time." THE LATE, GREAT STEVE ALLEN

"Reviewer's choice! A marvelous compendium. One of the best resources around." THE MIDWEST BOOK REVIEW'S INTERNET BOOKWATCH

"You'll find so many ideas in *How to Enjoy Your Retirement* [that] boredom won't be one of your choices. . . . An alphabetical guide offering a wide range of pastimes, with options appealing to both women and men . . . This user-friendly guide can help you make the most of the opportunities retirement brings. To help you follow up on the activity ideas, you'll find phone numbers, websites, and mailing addresses of resources to contact." VIM & VIGOR MAGAZINE

"Imaginative, informative, and playful . . . A winner!" SO YOUNG NEWSLETTER

"Retirement is near for many thousands of Americans, and this title is self-help for those who wonder, What will I do after I retire? Here are over 1000 ideas for new interests and activities to enrich those retirement years. Presented in alphabetical order, hundreds of ideas will jostle minds into renewed creativity. . . . Appendixes cover a wide variety of supporting information about volunteering, grandchildren, travel, and additional resources. The index provides more access points. Public libraries will want to purchase." LIBRARY JOURNAL

"A fountain of information and ideas [that will make] extremely nice and appropriate presents for my friends and relatives who are retired or are near retirement." TOM YOOK, RETIRED VICE PRESIDENT OF FIRST NATIONAL BANK

"Feelings of depression, boredom, and reduced self-worth are eliminated with this new activities-packed idea book for retirees and soon-to-be-retirees. The book makes a nice retirement gift." SENIOR FOCUS NEWSPAPER

"*How to Enjoy Your Retirement* takes a distinctly different approach to presenting and considering activities, adding easily accessible ideas and charts." LEONARD J. HANSEN, "MAINLY FOR SENIORS," COPLEY NEWS SERVICE

HOW TO ENJOY YOUR RETIREMENT

ACTIVITIES FROM

A TO Z

3RD EDITION

Tricia Wagner • Barbara Day

VanderWyk & Burnham

Published by VanderWyk & Burnham
P.O. Box 2789, Acton, Massachusetts 01720

Publisher's Cataloging-in-Publication Data
Wagner, Tricia.
    How to enjoy your retirement : activities from A to Z / Tricia Wagner, Barbara Day.—3rd ed.
        p.   cm.
    Includes bibliographical references and index.
    ISBN-13: 978-1-889242-28-6 (pbk.)
    ISBN-10: 1-889242-28-4 (pbk.)
    1. Retirement—United States—Miscellanea. 2. Aged—Recreation—United States—Miscellanea. 3. Creative activities and seat work. I. Day, Barbara. II. Wagner, Tricia. How to enjoy retirement. III. Title.
HQ1063.2.U6W34
646.7'9—dc21

Book design and health icon created by Dinardo Design
Pages 195–202 illustrations © Lenice Strohmeier

Manufactured in the United States of America
10 9 8 7 6 5 4 3 2 1

In loving memory
of Jerry Day
and John Day

CONTENTS

AUTHORS' PREFACE

hen the idea first came to us to write this book, retirement ideas flowed freely. The Internet was a foreboding, scary place because the concept was brand new. Now we don't know what we would do without it. What an awesome resource! And thanks to the response from our readers, we've progressed to this third edition of *How to Enjoy Your Retirement: Activities from A to Z*. Color has been added to the pages and, in keeping with our ever-changing world and the resource-rich nature of this book, we have updated references to previously listed websites, locations, and phone numbers and have added many more websites in context. It's easier than ever to check out a new interest that will help make your retirement more rewarding and fulfilling.

The late Steve Allen had great praise for *How to Enjoy Your Retirement* when he wrote the following: "Since humans vary so greatly in their tastes, I assume there can be no such thing as one simple retirement plan that will be best for all. What the authors of this wise and entertaining work have done is save the rest of us a good deal of study time. They have thought long and carefully, and consulted the views of others, about this issue of finding ourselves with 'nothing to do'; we would be smart to heed their advice and to consider the options they hold out."

How to Enjoy Your Retirement represents the combined efforts, ideas, and experiences, not only of ourselves, but also of friends, family members, and neighbors who eagerly provided us with additional ideas for the book. Thank you to all, and to those sources acknowledged later, who graciously allowed us to use quotations and excerpts from their works. This book is written for both men and women. We avoid using the term *spouse* and instead use the terms *partner* and *significant other* because of the varied living arrangements in society today and our desire to include everyone.

We do need to ask for your understanding when you find out that a phone number has been disconnected or has a new area code, a company's mail-forwarding order has expired, a website no longer exists, a book has gone out of print—and so on. The world will keep changing in between editions of this book, but we'll try to keep up! You can help by letting us know any time you learn of a fact in this book that is no longer applicable. Write to us c/o VanderWyk & Burnham, P.O. Box 2789, Acton, MA 01720. We also wish to mention that we have no relationship with any of the sites or businesses mentioned. We merely selected those that seemed to offer something appropriate to help get you started in an area that interests you.

We thoroughly enjoyed putting this book together. By no means do we pretend to have covered everything. We offer just a sprinkling of what's out there. We hope these ideas will contribute to happy and fulfilling retirement "careers" for our readers. It is truly exciting when we get feedback from readers. We've started a new Appendix (letter I) to begin recording some of the notes about real-life retirement experiences we've received.

Finally, in acknowledgment, we would like to thank Meredith Rutter, our publisher at VanderWyk & Burnham, and our editors Pat Moore and Pam Seastrand, for their enthusiasm, expertise, and guidance in bringing this project to completion and making it a reality. Also, for the kind permission to use material from the following sources, we thank Paul and Gail Dennison for *Brain Gym*®, Edu-Kinesthetics, Inc., P.O Box 3395, Ventura, CA 93006; *Denver Post*, 1560 Broadway, Denver, CO 80202; and the websites www.creativequotations.com and www.quotationspage.com.

INTRODUCTION

Y ou have worked somewhere between ten and fifty years, and RETIRE-MENT looms ahead. People face retirement with a variety of feelings, including excitement, anxiety, fear, and trepidation. If you have hobbies, you may be able to slip into retirement without missing a beat. If you do not have an all-consuming hobby, you may need some new interests and activities to enrich your retirement hours.

That's where this book comes into your life. These pages contain hundreds of ideas and activities, presented in alphabetical order, to jostle your mind into renewed creativity. Before you get to the *A* to *Z* of it, read the advice on taking a personal inventory of your retirement needs and desires (see section on next page). Also think about the importance of getting along with a significant other if you will now be together a lot more. Read the communication tips on pages 7–12.

The book's larger *A* to *Z* section—"Get in the Swing with These"— describes hundreds of ideas in varying degrees of detail (pages 13–112). If you're determined to stay physically healthy, look for the health icon that appears next to appropriate ideas in this section. Once warmed up by the "Swing" ideas, you can "Let Your Imagination Soar" with the next *A* to *Z* section: a smorgasbord of bare-bones topics to stimulate additional activity ideas (pages 113–181).

The first appendix (pages 183–188) provides the questions for taking a personal inventory. Remaining appendices explore the possibilities of spending time with your grandchildren (pages 189–193), doing exercises to synchronize your body and your brain (pages 195–203), starting a small business (pages 205–208), volunteering in your community or around the world (pages 209–214), and traveling afar (pages 215–238). Additional information resources (pages 239–248) and reading suggestions (pages 249–252) and some real-life retirement stories (pages 253–254) are also included.

We hope, by the power of suggestion, to enable you to plumb the depths of your mind and soul, to awaken the real you, to energize the creative mind that perhaps has lain dormant until this time in your life. Use this book as your private retirement planner. Only you can answer the questions and make the choices. If this is your own copy, there is plenty of space to jot down comments and note any sparks of interest. *How to Enjoy Your Retirement: Activities from A to Z* is as close to a magic formula as you can find. You may be surprised how many of these ideas blossom into meaningful and rewarding activities. It's all up to you!

Taking a Personal Inventory

Why do a personal inventory? Why not? Retirement is an ending and a beginning. The personal inventory can be your preface to an exciting new life. If you honestly answer the questions in Appendix A, you will have a better understanding of your past and present support system, interests, and relationships; where you want to live; why you are retiring; how you are going to pay for retirement; and whether there are things or people needing repair or attention in your life.

In Appendix A, "Who Are You?" (pages 183–184) helps you to explore your ancestry, family relationships, religion, leisure activities, and social connections. "What Have You Done? What Do You Do Well?" (page 184) explores talents and past successes. "When Will or Did You Retire?" (page 185) asks about your retirement schedule and your relationship with any significant other from the angle of perhaps being together a lot more now. "Where Will You Live?" (pages 185–186) raises the possibility of a move and travel plans. "Why Are You Retiring?" (page 186) explores your reason(s) for retirement and any special considerations you may have. "How Will You Pay for Retirement?" (pages 186–187) assesses income sources and options. "Determining Your Net Worth" (pages 187–188) reviews your assets and debts to identify exactly what you have to work with financially.

Overall, your inventory may introduce you to another you, one who has been repressed or overlooked for years. Wake up the real you! You are on the brink of a new adventure called *retirement*. Dip your toes in the water. Take notes from pages 115–181 and turn them into your "wish list." Be inventive, playful, even frivolous. What do you really want? What do you want the rest/best of your life to be?

THE COMMODORE'S PRAYER

Lord, thou knowest better than I know myself that I am growing older and will someday be old. Keep me from the fatal habit of thinking I must say something on every subject and on every occasion. Release me from craving to straighten out everybody's affairs. Make me thoughtful but not moody, helpful but not bossy. With my vast store of wisdom, it seems a pity not to use it all, but Thou knowest, Lord, that I want a few friends at the end.

Keep my mind free from the recital of endless details; give me wings to get to the point. Seal my lips on my aches and pains. They are increasing, and love of rehearsing them is becoming sweeter as the years go by. I dare not ask for grace enough to enjoy the tales of others' pains, but help me to endure them with patience.

I dare not ask for improved memory but for a growing humility and a lessening cocksureness when my memory seems to clash with the memories of others. Teach me the glorious lesson that occasionally I may be mistaken.

Keep me reasonably sweet; I do not want to be a Saint—some of them are so hard to live with—but a sour old person is one of the crowning works of the devil. Give me the ability to see good things in unexpected places and talents in unexpected people. And give me, Lord, the grace to tell them so. Amen.

Author Unknown

GETTING ALONG WITH EACH OTHER: COMMUNICATION TIPS

Many years ago, a friend and coworker gave Tricia some advice on how to communicate with colleagues. We have found the advice so effective, both at work and in personal relationships, that we want to share it with you in this section of communication tips.

Suppose somebody has made a mistake on something they have written. You know they've done it wrong, but you also know people are likely to be offended when told bluntly, "You've made a mistake here. This is wrong!" A more tactful comment might be, "Am I reading this right?" or "Would you explain this to me?" or "This doesn't seem quite right to me. Is there something I'm missing?" This approach gives the other person a chance to correct the mistake without feeling personally attacked.

To see the possibilities of tactful communication in a personal relationship, think about driving—often a source of conflict for couples. Imagine that you and your partner are in a car, and your partner is driving. Neither of you has ever been where you're heading, and you know that your partner is likely to get lost but hates to be told how to drive. So you might raise the question early: "What's the best way to get there?" Together you can discuss the best route for the time of day or conditions. Then about five blocks before it's time to turn and your car is in the wrong lane, ask, "Are we supposed to turn soon?" or "Is that our turn coming up?" This averts the possibly ugly consequences of driving by the turn. What you are doing is nudging without nagging or accusing.

O PROMISE ME

O promise me

That when the first intense excitement has died away, and the first bright luster of our association has dulled, you will recall that this was your idea as much as mine.

That you will always believe me to be the most desirable, and that the appearance of possession will not lull that desire into sleep.

That our dreams of a 'different' marriage can still come true, if we both but try, and keep on trying.

You will remember the time you said, "It takes two to quarrel," and I answered you, "Yes, and it takes two to get along."

You will once more meditate on the theories we expounded in soft, hushed tones—that marriage merely gave us an option on each other, and both of us would try to keep that option desirable above all things.

You will forever believe that those 'magic words' were truly magic, and while they granted no rights, they blessed and sanctioned our privileges.

You will never forget that I am just a human being, possessed of all the frailties and faults which love once glossed over.

You will never fail to grant me the kindnesses you extend so willingly to your most casual friends.

And that, as the years roll by, you will often say, I love you more—and more—and more.

As I have promised you.

Author Unknown

Know the difference between backseat driving and selective strategic navigating. Depending on the preference of the driver making a turn, it may be okay for the passenger to say, "You're fine on my side" or "You're clear after this red minivan." Sometimes it takes two to drive safely. Talk it over. If the driver doesn't want help, keep quiet unless there is danger of an accident.

Is one member of your household tidy and one member messy? Retirement can bring on arguments about how tidy the house needs to be. Just remember that neither of you is likely to change completely. If each gives a little, maybe you can reach a happy medium. Also, identify the chores you each like to do, and share all the other jobs around the house.

If both you and your significant other are retired, you may be spending much more time together than you did before retirement. Hopefully, clear, considerate communication has been an important part of your relationship all along. If not, problems may develop as the days go by. Sometimes one partner ends up spending time away from home just to stay out of the other person's way. Make it a priority to work out differences and reach resolutions before small conflicts grow into larger barriers between you. Discuss how much time you want to spend together and how much time you each want to spend alone or

L et there be spaces in your togetherness.

—Kahlil Gibran

with other friends. It can be miserable trying to occupy the same house all day every day without making some determination about togetherness. We firmly believe that as long as the two of you work together, you can work wonders. When you work against each other, everything falls apart.

If your partner is still working outside the home, he or she may have special needs, such as more spending money or fewer household responsibilities. On the other hand, if your partner is also retired or has

GOLDEN RULES FOR EASIER LIVING

1. If you open it, close it.

2. If you turn it on, turn it off.

3. If you unlock it, lock it up.

4. If you break it, admit it.

5. If you can't fix it, call in someone who can.

6. If you borrow it, return it.

7. If you value it, take care of it.

8. If you make a mess, clean it up.

9. If you move it, put it back.

10. If it belongs to someone else and you want to use it, get permission.

11. If you don't know how to operate it, leave it alone.

12. If it's none of your business, don't ask questions.

13. If it ain't broke, don't fix it.

14. If it will brighten someone's day — SAY IT!

Author Unknown

been home all along, you both will have adjustments to make now that you are home full-time, too.

Regarding busy work, it's amazing how things to do will expand to fill up the time available. Make sure you really need or want to do all these things and are not just finding busy work.

Also, avoid speaking for your partner. For example, don't say, "I'm sure Bill will be happy to work on your car" (or whatever) when Bill may have a dozen other things he would rather be doing. Check with the other person first. You might say, "He keeps pretty busy now that he's retired" or "She keeps her own schedule. I'll ask her." Don't volunteer your significant other's time or services without checking first.

Both parties need to know how to shop for groceries, do the wash, operate the microwave, write checks, balance the checkbook, and manage investments. Both parties need to know about the cars, maintenance schedules, location of keys and titles, all insurance policies, each other's valuable collections, lawn equipment, jewelry, discharge papers, wills and living wills (which you should carry with you when you travel), final wishes, and funeral plans.

When speaking to each other, particularly in the presence of others, try to avoid using harsh voice inflections. Discuss your dissatisfactions in private and try to come to understandings that will work for both of you. Keep in mind the maxim, "It's not what you say, it's how you say it."

If you need help developing communication skills in your relationship, don't be afraid to seek assistance, whether it be through joining a program at your place of worship, reading books or listening to tapes on communication and relationships, or going to a professional counselor. Good communication between you and your significant other will definitely enhance your retirement.

Once a woman has forgiven her man, she must not reheat his sins for breakfast.

—Marlene Dietrich

Finally, have consideration for the memory lapses, foibles, idiosyncrasies, and infirmities we all have that may become more pronounced as we grow older.

A true conception of the relation of the sexes will not admit of conqueror and conquered; it knows of but one great thing: to give one's self boundlessly in order to find oneself richer, deeper and better.

—Emma Goldman

GET IN THE SWING WITH THESE

ACTIVITIES FROM

A TO Z

Adopt a Highway — Colorado has a wonderful volunteer program through which groups of people clean litter from the highways. Contact your state's highway maintenance office to see if they have such a program. Inquire about starting one (1-800-200-0003 or www.adoptahighway.com).

Adopt-A-Native-Elder — Necessities like food and clothing have been delivered to nearly 500 Navajo elders in remote parts of southern Utah and northern Arizona. These elders can be "adopted" by volunteers and helped financially with such things as propane, warm clothing, groceries, and electricity bills. One elder likes to garden, so his sponsor sends him seeds. Another elder's grandchildren are about the same age as her sponsor's children, so that sponsor sends "hand-me-down" clothing as her own children outgrow still-good clothes. Some of the elders sell quilts or other crafts made with donated materials. An annual benefit Rug Show is held in Park City, Utah. If interested in participating, contact Adopt-A-Native-Elder Program, P.O. Box 3401, Park City, UT 84060 (or call 1-435-649-0535 or visit www.anelder.org).

Adoption Open Records — Find your long-lost relatives. Try OmniTrace at www.omnitrace.com (people search experts) and Bastard Nation at www.bastards.org (adoptee rights organization). Good luck and have fun!

Aging Family Members — If you are worried about or caring for an aging family member, the following are helpful sources of information: *Are Your Parents Driving You Crazy? Getting to Yes with Competent Aging Parents, Second Edition*, by Joseph A. Ilardo, PhD, LCSW and Carole R. Rothman, PhD (VanderWyk & Burnham); *The Baby Boomer's Guide to Caring for Your Aging Parent* by Gene Williams (Taylor Trade Publishing); *How to Care for Aging Parents, Second Edition* by Virginia Morris (Workman Publishing Co.). The website www.caregiver.com is written for caregivers. They also have a magazine titled *Today's Caregiver*, which is very useful.

Airplanes — The next time you make a flight reservation, think about the direction you'll be traveling. Try to reserve a seat on the shady side of the plane to avoid the sun's glare.

Alcohol and Drugs — Request publications or videotapes, and get information organized by drug type and audience from the National Clearing House for Alcohol and Drug Information, 1-800-729-6686, www.health.org.

Alzheimer's Disease — Get fact sheets, a caregiver resource list, and local support group information by contacting the Alzheimer's Disease Education and Referral Center (ADEAR) at 1-800-438-4380, www.alzheimers.org. Find additional information through the Alzheimer's Association at 1-800-272-3900, www.alz.org; and the John Douglas French Alzheimer's Foundation 1-310-445-4656, www.jdfaf.org.

Americans Age 50 and Over — Join AARP (www.aarp.org) and enjoy the many benefits it offers. This includes annual subscriptions to the

AARP Bulletin and *AARP The Magazine*. Computer users can receive news and information about the association and share opinions and views. Call the AARP membership center at 1-888-OUR-AARP (687-2277) or visit that section of their website. For group health insurance plans, call 1-800-874-0626 x FH2 (www.aarphealthcare.com). For investment program information call 1-800-958-6457 (www.aarpfunds.com).

Animation/Computer Skills — Draw digital animated characters with a computer. You may discover a marketable skill, and Hollywood may want you! Places to look for jobs include Sony Pictures Imageworks, Klasky Csupo, HBO Animation, Walt Disney Television Animation, Nickelodeon's Nicktoons, Industrial Light & Magic, and Pixar Animation Studios. For company addresses, check the information desk at your local library for *American Business Directory* or the *Million Dollar Directory*. Also, you could check ads in current animation magazines, or contact the Animation Industry Database at www.aidb.com.

Aquariums — What could be more fun or relaxing than a beautiful aquarium in your own home? For complete aquarium systems, including the stand, lights, and filters (all you need to add are the fish), contact MMFI, P.O. Box 37531, Denver, CO 80237, or call 1-303-478-7093. Their website at www.aquaricare.com includes an information package you can download. These aquarium systems use a new filter design called algae scrubbers and have a surging device that makes waves in the aquarium. They manufacture a broad range of equipment to create aquarium conditions that rival nature.

Archaeological Dig—At thousands of sites throughout the U.S., archaeologists uncover delicate and ancient artifacts from America's past. Volunteers of all ages are often welcome to help. To find a dig near you, contact your state historical society or request the Archaeological Fieldwork Opportunities Bulletin, a publication of the Archaeological Institute of America, Department AFOB, 656 Beacon Street, Fourth Floor, Boston, MA 02215 (1-617-353-9361, www.archaeology.org).

Archery—Take up archery as a hobby (www.pse-archery.com).

Art—Have you always had a love of art? Visit art museums and art exhibits. Start collecting art. Study art history. Visit www.art.com.

New artists must break a hole in the subconscious and go fishing there.

—Robert B. Hall

Art Car Weekend—Attend an Art Car Weekend, held in Houston in May. People paint their cars to represent everything from fruits and vegetables to dreamy, celestial, glow-in-the-dark murals. Often, the artists dress to match their cars. One man has a long-horned steer for a hood ornament. He says, "When I pass a pasture, even the cows look up." For more information, call Houston's Chamber of Commerce (1-713-844-3600) or visit www.artcars.com.

Art Gallery on Wheels—Create an art gallery on wheels. One man turned his minivan into an art gallery, removing seats and installing a second battery for lighting the art. Van Go Mobile Arts Inc. delivers constructive activities to children at risk for drug and alcohol use, teen pregnancy, truancy, or delinquency (www.van-go.org).

Artifacts—Study the artifacts of North America. Some that have been discovered in several sites near the Wisconsin-Illinois line may be as old as or predate Mayan artifacts found in Monte Verde, Chile. Other old sites include Clovis, New Mexico; Meadowcroft, near Pittsburgh—

the site of a rock shelter some believe was used by hunters 19,000 years ago; and the Yukon Territory's Old Crow site, where archaeologists dug up bone tools that could be 27,000 years old. Contact the archaeology department in a local college or state university or inquire at the library. Also, visit www. americanartifacts.com/smma.

Artists — Do you work with watercolor, oils, acrylics, or mixed media? Enter your artwork in a juried art competition, such as the September National Show held in Cheyenne, Wyoming. The deadline for your entry is in July. For a prospectus, send a #10 self-addressed, stamped envelope to Cheyenne Artists Guild, 1701 Morrie Avenue, Cheyenne, WY 82001 or call 1-307-632-2263. If there's not a show in your area, why not start one?

Arts and Crafts Worldwide — Buy handmade, one-of-a-kind items, made by craftspeople in more than thirty Third World countries, at a Ten Thousand Villages shop. They have banana-fiber animals from Kenya; colorful, handwoven table linens from India; Indonesian shadow puppets; and oversized blue-and-white Vietnamese flowerpots. This shop, found in different cities, is a nonprofit store staffed by volunteers. Call 1-717-859-8100 or visit www.tenthousandvillages.org to see if there's a store near you. Also visit the website of Global Exchange at www.gxonlinestore.org to learn about their Fair Trade Program and offerings from other countries. Global Exchange is headquartered in San Francisco; call 1-800-505-4410.

Astronomers — Become a backyard astronomer, and network with the Center for Backyard Astrophysics, founded with the help of the National Science Foundation and run under the direction of Columbia University (http://cba.phys.columbia.edu/). The backyard astronomers record data and send it to CBA via computer. Hundreds of thousands of amateur astronomers worldwide belong to similar clubs. Some clubs have gone so far as to pool money to buy highly sophisticated equipment. For example, a man named Thomas Droege of Batavia, Illinois, spent $50,000 to build telescope cameras that he gave away to amateurs who joined his group of backyard observers. Also take a look at what the Amateur Astronomers Association is up to; visit www. aaa.org or call 1-212-535-2922 or write to Amateur Astronomers Association, Inc., Gracie Station, P.O. Box 383, New York, NY 10028.

Authors — Do you know any authors? Have area writers been featured in your local newspaper? Ask them to give a talk about their works. Charge a small admission to cover refreshments.

Autobiography — Would you like to write an autobiography? *The Book of Myself* by Carl and David Marshall (Hyperion) is a do-it-yourself book of 201 questions that prompt you to record your personal habits and traits, your history, your wisdom, and the stories you want to share with future generations. Answer the question on each page, and your story is told!

Automobile — If you want to get rid of a used vehicle, consider donating it to the Boys and Girls Clubs, which fix up and sell the cars to raise money to fund their programs. If automobiles interest you (as they do Tricia's husband, Bill, who provided this section), there are many ways to enjoy this hobby. You can get into detailing, which would require some training. Go to a detail shop and learn how they do it. Many shops are willing to share their trade secrets. You can buy, sell, or trade cars as a dealer or wholesaler. This may require working with a dealership as a salesperson for a period of time, or working with another wholesaler. You can collect cars or join a car club (see below).

Collect Cars: Buy and sell collector vehicles. Trading collector cars successfully requires some schooling and research to learn the market. Several useful publications, such as *Hemmings Motor News, Old Cars Weekly,* and others, are available at newsstands. Getting started also might require an outlay of between $3,000 and $100,000. To learn more about collector cars, become acquainted with a person in the old-car hobby who is willing to teach you. Attend some old-car auctions, just to watch and listen. It takes time to become familiar with the market. Contact *Hemmings Motor News* at P.O. Box 100, Bennington, VT 05201; 1-800-227-4373, ext. 550; or www.hemmings.com. *Old Cars Weekly* is published by Krause Publications, Inc., 700 East State Street, Iola, WI 54990; call 1-800-258-0929 or go online to www.krause.com/static/cars.htm.

Kruse (not Krause) Auctions hold collector-car auctions all over the country throughout the year. For a free brochure of the Kruse Auctions, or to sell a collector car, write to P.O. Box 190, 5540 C.R. 11-A, Auburn, IN 46706, or call 1-800-968-4444. Visit them online at www.kruse.com. Also visit www.barrett-jackson.com, or call 1-480-421-6694.

Car Clubs: Join a car club if you own just about any car made before 1970. Pick from the Horseless Carriage Club, the Falcon Club, or the Thunderbird Club. There are the Studebaker, Early V-8, Model-T, and Corvette Clubs, and hundreds of others. Members have fun with car-related activities and social events. Contact a dealership that sells your kind of car. They probably know of a related car club. Activities are sometimes listed in local newspapers, or try the telephone book Yellow Pages under *Clubs*. Visit www.greatrace.com for information about a unique "timed endurance rally-race." If you're going to store an old car for any length of time, add gas stabilizer to the gas tank and put moth balls and D-Con around to keep mice from eating your wiring and upholstery.

Automobile Insurance—To get online insurance quotes from 200 companies and further consumer information regarding insurance, contact www.insure.com/health/individual.html. Also included is information regarding consumer complaints against insurers.

Automobile Lamp—Buy a beautiful and unique lamp made from an automobile crankshaft. Each lamp is different and a conversation piece as well as a piece of art. Call Campbell Levy Designs at 303-762-7936 or visit www.campbelllevydesigns.com.

B

Babyography—Order a "Babyography," a distinctive keepsake for your grandchild's room. It contains a dozen facts about the baby's birth, including date, time, weight, length, hair color, doctor's name, and parents' names, as well as the child's astrological sign, names of other famous people who share the child's birthday, and a time capsule of current headlines. Call 1-805-373-5197, write to P.O. Box 1648, Thousand Oaks, CA 91358, or e-mail info@allbaby.com for a free brochure. More information can be found at www.allbaby.com.

Back Trouble—If you have trouble with your back, order a catalog from BackSaver, 3000 East Imperial Highway, Lynwood, CA 90262 (or call 1-800-251-2225). In the Washington, DC, area visit JoAnne's Bed and Back shops. In nine or so states the Healthy Back Stores are helpful (www.betterback.com). Also, Relax the Back stores are located throughout the United States and Canada.

Baldness—Shop for baldness remedies. Choices include Propecia, Rogaine, Kevis, and more. You can talk to a Kevis consultant at 1-800-510-7068. Learn more about hair loss and treatment options at www.newhairgrowth.com, www.folica.com/regrowth/rogaine, and www.medicalhairrestoration.com.

Bed and Breakfast—For bed-and-breakfast information in Europe, call 1-800-872-2632. Their website is www.londonbandb.com, with links to other cities in Europe. Their bed-and-breakfast lodging is the equivalent of a three-star hotel rating. For bed-and-breakfast information worldwide, check www.bedandbreakfast.com. If you enjoy meeting people and don't mind putting yourself into your work, consider owning and operating your own bed-and-breakfast inn, which can be a very interesting business.

Beer—Open a brew pub of your own, or just create your own family recipe. Visit www.realbeer.com.

Bird Hunting/Watching—Get a good dog and a few friends and go on a bird hunting trip. If you're interested in bird watching, join the National Audubon Society. Read the book *All the Birds of North America,* a field guide beautifully designed and written by Jack Griggs for the American Bird Conservancy (Collins/HarperCollins). In this book, illustrations are grouped under color-coded icons representing the birds' feeding behavior and easily recognizable features. You may want to install bird feeders in your yard. Stock the feeders with black-oil type sunflower, white proso millet, niger or thistle seed, suet, or fruit. Become a member of the National Bird-Feeding Society, www.birdfeeding.org. Membership includes the *Wild Bird News* newsletter. Their website provides a wealth of information on how to be a better bird feeder.

Birth Order — Study the interesting hypotheses presented in *Born to Rebel: Birth Order, Family Dynamics and Creative Lives* by Frank J. Sulloway (reprint edition by Vintage). He describes the different traits and behavior patterns characteristic of first-born, middle-born, and later-born children. Do you and people you know fit his profiles?

Book Club — Start or join a book club to read and discuss books every month. Eating and socializing can be part of this wonderful pastime.

Life-transforming ideas have always come to me through books.

—bell hooks

Book Storage — Follow the lead of the Library of Congress and increase your book storage space by one-third: Sort books by their sizes so shelves can be raised or lowered. The Library of Congress (www.loc.gov) also gives away thousands of duplicate or unneeded books to nonprofit groups. You have to travel to the Washington, DC, library to select the books. Write to the Library of Congress, Surplus Books Program, James Madison Memorial Building, 101 Independence Avenue SE, Room B-03, Washington, DC 20540 (phone 1-202-707-9524).

Books and Tapes for the Blind — The National Library Service for the Blind and Physically Handicapped produces recorded and Braille books and magazines. Of the thirty to forty million Americans over sixty-five, many are temporarily or permanently unable to read print. They now have access to about 700,000 biographies, bestsellers, classics, mysteries, romance novels, and poetry books. Joe Volz, with the *Maturity News Service,* writes: "The talking books and magazines are narrated by professionals and produced on cassette tapes or flexible disc records. Local libraries lend out the books, along with easy-to-use equipment. Readers can participate directly from home by postage-free mail. Books and equipment are all loaned free, and easy-to-operate machines are also loaned free." To be connected with the library serving your area call 1-888-NLS-READ (657-7323).

Books on Tape—Can't find the time to read the latest bestseller? Listen to an audiobook while driving, jogging, or walking. Call 1-800-638-1304 (www.recordedbooks.com) for more information about books on tape. Many libraries and bookstores carry audiobooks. Also visit www.audiotogo.com (1-847-381-9900) and www.booksontape.com.

Boredom—Fight boredom by trying something new. Maybe you'll like it!

Braille Printing—Donate or raise money to buy computers to help speed braille printing done in Boston, Massachusetts; Chicago, Illinois; Louisville, Kentucky; Stewart, Florida; and the Jenny Beck Braille Center in Philadelphia, Pennsylvania. The Beck Center uses these computers, which have revolutionized the printing process. At some locations, printing can be slow and laborious, done on just a six-key typewriter called a Braillewriter. For more information, contact the Braille Institute of America at 1-800-BRAILLE (272-4553) or visit their website at www.brailleinstitute.org.

Brainstorm—Do this with others to find something to do. That's the way this book got started. One little comment—"What will I do when I retire?"—took fire and turned into this book.

Bridge—Play bridge. It's a wonderful way to meet people and stimulate your brain. Go to www.okbridge.com or www.acbl.org to play bridge live with others.

Bug Zapper—Throw away your bug zapper. It kills more good bugs than it kills biting bugs, according to a study by the University of Delaware at Newark, New Jersey. Buzz Off™ clothing repels bugs (www.exofficio.com or 1-800-644-7303).

Build—Build a child's or an adult's self-esteem; a patio, a window box, a birdbath, or a tree house; a path in the woods; momentum for a cherished cause; a PowerPoint (computerized) presentation.

To love what you do and feel that it matters—how could anything be more fun?

—Katharine Graham

Build a Bear—Build-a-Bear Workshops are located all over the world with new stores opening all the time. You can choose various holiday themes, clothing, and accessories for your special bear recipient. Call 1-877-789-BEAR (2327) or go to www.buildabear.com.

Bumper Stickers—Enjoy deciphering license plates and reading bumper stickers. Paul Rosa decided the latter were too safe and too boring. He dreamed up some satire on wheels with his first sticker, "My Kid Beat Up Your Honor Student." Rosa's bumper sticker sold at the rate of 40,000 per year through a national gift store chain. With your own ideas, visit www.absorbentprinting.com (1-866-618-3471) for personalized, business, or political campaign bumper stickers.

Bungee Jumping—It's free in some places for those over seventy years of age. Interested at any age? See www.bungee.com/bzapp.

Butter Is Better, or Is It?—There are two schools of thought on this one! Check with your doctor before deciding "to butter or not to butter." Butter substitute products that claim to reduce cholesterol are Benecol, Take Control, and Smart Balance.

C

Camp for Blind Kids—Become involved in National Camps for Blind Children, 4444 S. 52nd Street, Lincoln, NE 68516 (1-402-488-0981, www.christianrecord.org). For non-denominational see www.acb.org/resources/sports.html.

Camping—Take either short trips or extended camping excursions. Enjoy the campgrounds when they're not crowded with holiday and weekend campers. Visit www.camping.com.

Cancer—Change your diet and you can potentially escape some cancers. Increase your intake of fruits and vegetables. Stop smoking, keep your weight down, and limit your alcohol intake to only one or two small drinks a day. If you are a licensed cosmetologist or hairdresser, you can give makeup suggestions, skin and nail care tips, and ideas on how to wear wigs and scarves to women undergoing chemotherapy or radiation and coping with hair loss. This program was founded by the Cosmetic, Toiletry, and Fragrance Association, supported by the National Cosmetology Association and the American Cancer Society. Call 1-800-395-LOOK (5665).

Candles—Use candles for something besides lighting or romance. Now people are using candles for everything from home decor and aromatherapy to meditation and spiritual practice. A retail and mail order store called Illuminations has everything from white votive candles to large, colored aromatherapy pillars. Call 1-800-621-2998 or visit www.illuminations.com. Coventry Creations, a company-based shop in Ferndale, Michigan, makes a line of candles that contain herbs, oils, and blessings. For more information, call 1-800-810-3837 or visit www.coventrycreations.com. Some say that lighting a candle is a way of letting go, of giving yourself permission to get rid of negativity.

Cane—If you need to use a cane, how about a clear plastic cane you can insert something decorative into? Comfort Design sells clear canes that contain anything from tiny silk roses to fishing flies. The cane handles are made with a special process to withstand up to 300 pounds and not break. Consider a "Convertible Cane™," which has a tip that can be removed and the decoration inside changed. Call Tom Wilson, President, at 1-888-547-6240. You may also want to ask him about the "Golden Retriever" for help with picking things up off the floor.

Carp—Along the Mississippi River, fish markets sell smoked carp, carp jerky, and even carp bologna. Carp are also great sport fish. Join the Carp Anglers Group, 3804 Yacht Club Dr., Arlington, TX 76016 and learn their "secrets" for carp fishing. The toll-free number is 1-888-CARP118 (227-7118). Take a look at their photo gallery at www.carpanglersgroup.com.

Casket—Buy your casket while you're still living. Here are four sources for selecting caskets or urns directly: Direct Casket (East Coast 1-800-732-2753, West Coast 1-800-772-2753, www.directcasket.com); Tribute Direct (1-800-994-3070, www.tributedirect.com); Casket XPress (1-800-550-7262, www.casketxpress.com); Urn XPress (1-800-550-1172, www.urnxpress.com).

Castles/Churches — Buy a vacant castle or church in Britain, France, Amsterdam, Netherlands, Germany, or elsewhere in the world. Convert it into a library, a shop, a cultural center, an apartment, or a discotheque. Visit the Castles of the World website, www.castles.org, or see www.castles-for-sale.com.

Cellular Phones — Check out the cellular phone world. All kinds of phones and plans can be found in electronic stores, through your local phone company, and even in the supermarket. The plans vary as to monthly rates, time-of-day restrictions, and price per minute. The phones themselves range in size from fairly lightweight to almost weightless. In an emergency, your cell phone can be priceless.

> The cure for boredom is curiosity. There is no cure for curiosity.
>
> —Dorothy Parker

Ceramics/Paint Bar — Buy clean, white, bisque ceramic houseware items in a paint bar. Paint them into masterpieces of your own, and the paint bar will fire and glaze the items for you. Schedule a special time at a paint bar with your friends to make a whole dinner set, or whatever you want to make. Many places have paint plans for groups and children.

Chatty Cathy — Get your Chatty Cathy doll fixed by e-mailing Chatty Cathy's Haven at KDM913@aol.com. Join a Chatty Cathy Collectors Club by contacting editor Melissa Gilkey Mince, P.O. Box 4426, Seminole, FL 33775. Learn little known facts about Chatty Cathy dolls at www.ttinet.com/chattycathy.

Checklist for Leaving the House — Make a verbal or written checklist for leaving the house. If you're getting more absent-minded (and most of us do as we age), you'll be glad you have a checklist. Before leaving the house, have you turned everything off — the iron, the lights, the stove? Have you turned everything on — the alarm system, the lights, a radio —

whatever you use for security? Do you have everything you need—money, keys (house and car), gas in the car, whatever you're taking with you (present, prizes, potluck dish, clothing, tickets), directions and a phone number for where you're going? Did you plan your round trip logically to save gas and time? Do you need to stop somewhere on the way? Do you need to pick somebody up? What about on the way back?

Childcare—Helping out in a childcare center for a business near you might be interesting part-time work. Ask what licensing or training you may need.

Children—Take your favorite little ones to a petting zoo. Fix them up with Halloween costumes and go out trick-or-treating. Encourage any talents the children demonstrate. You will be drawn together when you attend their baptisms, their First Communions, and their graduations. Go to their ball games and cheer for them, ache for them in their hurts, and celebrate with them their victories. Being with children can show us how to play again, how to laugh and hug. Take a look also at Appendix B, Spending Time with Grandchildren.

 Chinese Medicine—Learn about traditional Chinese therapies, including acupuncture. Some insurance companies cover acupuncture. For information, visit the website at www.acupuncture.com.

Chocolate—Enjoy a chocolate bar! For your information, dark chocolate contains the least amount of fat. Try www.chocolate.com.

City and County Governments—Volunteer in the planning and zoning department of your city or county government, or work as a school crossing guard.

A *great marriage is not when the 'perfect couple' comes together. It is when an imperfect couple learns to enjoy their differences.*

—Dave Meurer

Clean House Naturally—Make homemade products for doing easy, cheap, and toxic-free cleaning. Get *Clean House, Clean Planet* by Karen Logan (Simon & Schuster). She gives recipes using basic ingredients like club soda, olive oil, vinegar, and baking soda, which do not contribute to indoor air pollution. She advises against concocting your own recipes because mixing two safe ingredients may give unsafe results. You can also contact a Shaklee (www.shaklee.com) or similar distributor for environmentally safe cleaning products. Sun & Earth (www.sunandearth.com) products are available at natural food stores, supermarkets, and drug chains.

Climbing Wall—Climbing walls are great for fun and exercise. They can be found at sporting goods stores, many recreation centers, and cruise ships. You can also build one yourself. Call To The Top at 1-800-965-0590 or visit www.tothetopwalls.com.

Closets—Clean out your closets. Consider having them professionally organized by a company specializing in closets. Surf the Web or take a look at books such as *Unclutter Your Home* by Donna Smallin (Storey Publishing) and *Clear Your Clutter with Feng Shui* by Karen Kingston (Broadway Books).

Clothing—Sort through your clothing. Once retired, you won't need many power suits. Consider selling them at a near-new shop. They must be clean and in style. Start whittling down your wardrobe before retirement if possible. Think of all the money you'll save on dry cleaning. Shop for your new, casual, washable clothes at discount stores, thrift shops, and garage sales. Did you throw your shirts away when you lost a button? No more. Keep your clothes in good repair. Sew on buttons and mend rips before they become huge. If you are a dancer or like parties, you'll want some nice clothes. If you need a suit for a special occasion, rent one from the same place you rent formal wear.

When it's all over, it's not who you were . . . it's whether you made a difference.

—Bob Dole

Clowning— Learn to be a clown. It can be lots of fun. Join the Shriners' clown group or be independent. Entertain at children's parties. Can you do magic tricks? Can you twist balloons into doggies? Do you enjoy children? If you love making people laugh and you enjoy traveling, visit www.sunniebunniezz.com/clowning or www.clownsofamerica.org.

Clubs— Join Kiwanis, Rotary International, the Republicans or the Democrats, a car club, a book club, etc.

Coaching— Coach children's sports teams. Local schools and city parks and recreation departments are always looking for volunteers to coach different sporting events for kids.

Coffee— This is big right now, especially fancy coffees. Is it too late to open a coffee shop or coffee house? Would it be feasible? Would it be profitable? Would it be fun?

Collecting— People collect all sorts of things, from souvenir spoons to roosters to antiques to collector cars, and the list is endless! There are books available for most hobbies to help you with your collection. Following is just a taste of the collecting world.

Antique Collecting: Antiques can be fun to collect, refurbish, use, buy, sell, auction, and look for everywhere. Collecting antiques can also be profitable. For more information about antiques, check your local library for books on this subject. Search for interesting stuff at www.curioscape.com. Check the newspaper for scheduled antique shows, and watch "Antiques Roadshow" on TV.

Doll Houses and Miniatures: Take a class at the largest miniatures and dollhouse shop in New England: Earth and Tree Miniatures (www.dollhouse-miniatures.com), 276 Route 101, #1, Amherst, New Hampshire 03031 (to preregister: 1-877-801-8707).

Toys: Collecting toys is a popular and growing hobby for people of all ages. Categories include cars, trucks, planes, and trains made from plastic, die cast, tin plate, and cast iron. Collecting toys is a fairly inexpensive hobby. Ask at your local hobby shop about clubs for toy collectors. They will probably have several publications, also. Most people collect the toys they loved and played with as children.

Collection Service—Start a debt collection service for doctors' offices, law firms, or other businesses.

Composing—Compose poetry, lyrics for music, a short story, or a novel. Try submitting your work to a local publication.

Computers—Everyone has at least one good story in them by just telling their own story. Computers make it possible to write and illustrate your story. Share with your family what your early life was like. Network throughout the world and stay in touch

Reading well is one of the great pleasures that solitude can afford you.

—Harold Bloom

regularly with friends and family via e-mail. To enhance your experience at the computer, refer to Appendix C, *Brain Gym®* Activities.

Concert/Symphony—Gather a group of friends together and attend a concert or symphony of your favorite group, singer, or orchestra. Take a class in music appreciation.

Cooking—Now you have time to prepare recipes you've been collecting over the years. This will add variety to those monotonous menus you might have used to save time in meal preparation while you were working. Bake homemade bread or make homemade ice cream. Do you have a special recipe for something that you could enter in cooking or baking contests? Could your product be marketed? Many people have had great marketing success with good family or ethnic recipes. Would you be interested in running a catering business? The Federal Food and Drug Administration, the U.S. Department of Agriculture, and several state agencies have rules and regulations about food production. Appendix D, Starting a Business, will provide you with some sources of information. Contact a local adult education program or technical college to inquire about taking, or teaching, a cooking class.

Cooking without Fat: An easy way to cut the fat in canned goods, soups, stews, and baked beans is to place the can in the refrigerator for thirty minutes before opening it, and then skim off the solidified fat. For a more creative approach while still down to earth for beginning cooks, empty-nesters, and health-oriented small families, pick up *Healthy Cooking for Two (or Just You)* by Frances Price (Rodale).

Food Dictionary: Browse through *Webster's New World Dictionary of Culinary Arts* by Sarah Labensky, Gaye Ingram, and Steve Labensky (Prentice Hall). Three years of research went into this project.

Vegetarian Cooking: *Heart Healthy Diets: The Vegetarian Way* describes inexpensive, low fat, high fiber foods and meal choices. Write to the Vegetarian Resource Group, P.O. Box 1463, Baltimore, MD 21203. It's free!

Coupons — Clip coupons. It doesn't take much of your time, and you can save a lot of money. If you've been doing this, you already know of the savings. Go a step further and exchange your unwanted coupons with other coupon clippers. Some supermarkets have special coupon-exchange areas. You'll get even more coupons that are useful to you, and that adds up to more savings! Also, companies often send coupons to customers who call their toll-free number.

Crafts — Ideas abound for all kinds of crafts: sewing (dolls, stuffed animals, aprons, quilts, special clothing, to name a few), ceramics, wood-working, tole painting, flower arranging, knitting, crocheting, and many, many more! Crafting is a wonderful way to fill your time and nurture your creativity. Crafts can be sold, entered in craft shows, given as gifts, donated to fund raisers, or entered in various fair competitions for a chance at winning a ribbon. Barb once met a woman who loved to make a particular type of dressed bunny. Each bunny she made was different. She displayed the bunnies at a library and donated proceeds from the sale of her bunnies to buy books for the children's section. What a wonderful and unique idea! She was doing something that she loved and making a special contribution to her community, too. Readily available in supermarkets, home improvement stores, craft stores and drug stores are magazines filled with crafts and home decorating projects. Watch your local PBS station or home and garden channel for craft and decorating ideas.

Crime Novels — Read something written by Minette Walters, who not only writes crime novels but also visits criminals in prisons. Her books include

The Ice House, The Sculptress, The Scold's Bridle, The Dark Room, and *The Echo.*
She is fascinated by what has driven somebody to kill another person.

Cults — If you think you or someone you love is being targeted by
a cult, contact the International Cultic Studies Association (ICSA)
at 1-239-514-3081.

Dance, Dance, Dance — One of the best ways to improve your social
life, stay in good physical shape, and it's always great fun! Single men
who dance can become gentleman-hosts on some cruise lines as dance
partners for single ladies who otherwise would not have dance partners.

Dating — If you are interested in meeting someone with similar interests,
and perhaps romance, check out www.Meetup.com, organized for real-
world face-to-face gatherings called "Meetups" that usually occur at
least once a month. Also consider www.eHarmony.com. Good luck!

Debt — If in debt, establish a program to get out of debt. Guidelines
are provided here. The first set consists of three general rules.

1. Monthly payments for all debts combined should not exceed
   more than 40 percent of your pretax income.

2. Divide the price of your car or cars by the number of years you
   plan to use them. If that amount is more than 10 percent of
   your gross income, you are spending too much for the car(s).

3. Credit card payments should not exceed 12 percent of your income if you are a single-income family. On more than one income, you can safely have a 15 percent ratio. Credit card payments over 25 percent of your income signal serious trouble.

Here is another set of rules you might choose to follow:

1. Pay yourself first: 10 percent (provides a jingle in your pocket and allows for contingencies).

2. Debt payments should not exceed 20 percent of your after-tax income.

3. Living expenses should not exceed 70 percent of your after-tax income.

Whichever guidelines you choose to follow, the following strategies will help you manage your debt payments:

1. Make the largest payments on debts carrying the lowest interest. (You will pay more of the principal faster, and then you can consolidate the remaining debts with a lower-interest loan).

2. Use debt consolidation loans or home equity loans.

3. If interest rates allow you to refinance your mortgage, you can use the money saved each month to pay off debts.

Lead me not into temptation, I can find the way myself.

—Rita Mae Brown

4. Stop using credit cards.

5. Negotiate payment schedules with credit card companies, or negotiate lower interest rates.

6. If you are in danger of losing your house or car, or your bills are still out of line with what you can pay, downsize or sell your assets.

Delta Queen Trip—Take a trip on the Delta Queen or the Mississippi Queen. Live the legend of Mark Twain's Mississippi with a three- to twelve-night trip on an authentic "floating palace." Call for a free brochure at 1-800-543-1949 (or visit www.deltaqueen.com and www. vacationstogo.com/cruiseships/mississippiqueen.cfm).

Demonstrator—Be a demonstrator in a grocery store.

 Depression—Seek professional help in the form of a combination of antidepressant medication and psychiatry, which seem to work well together. For mild cases of depression, sometimes self-care will help. Put a little fun in your life by scheduling something you like to do at least once a week. Get together with others who are cheerful. See a movie, have lunch, play games or cards, have a massage, shop, take a walk. Try other kinds of exercise. Also, try to figure out what's bothering you. Sometimes medications or even food allergies can contribute to depression. Bright light therapy might help to improve the way you feel. Consider being a participant in a clinical trial for depression treatments by calling 1-877-5TRIALS (587-4257) or visiting www.veritasmedicine.com.

R*egret for the things we did can be tempered by time; it is regret for the things we did not do that is inconsolable.*

—Sidney J. Harris

Design—Design a sports arena, stadium, or uniform. Present your plans to the owner of the club or team.

Design Harmony—Learn about Feng Shui (pronounced "fung shway"), an ancient Oriental art of placement of objects and furniture so energy can be balanced or redirected. Take a class in Feng Shui or read one of the many books on the subject, for example, *Feng Shui with What You Have: Maximum Harmony, Minimum Effort* by Connie Spruill and Sylvia Watson (Adams Media Corporation).

Detectors—

Carbon Monoxide Detector: Buy one. Retail stores carry several brands, such as First Alert, American Sensors, Inc., Kidde, and the Nighthawk 2000. Low-level exposure to carbon monoxide gas can cause health problems in elderly people and children.

Radon Gas Detector: Check your basement for radon gas, which is the second leading cause of lung cancer in the United States. For more information, call the Environmental Protection Agency (EPA) in your state.

Smoke Detector: Change the battery in your smoke detector each time you adjust your clock for Daylight Saving Time.

Disabilities—Work with people with disabilities. Teach them to play golf or ski. You may want to volunteer with the Special Olympics, 1133 19th Street NW, Washington, DC 20036 (1-202-628-3630, www.specialolympics.org).

Documentary Films—Do you have an idea or the time or the desire to produce a documentary film? As a jumping off point, check with your library reference desk. Also look under *Video* or *Motion Picture Producers and Studios* in the Yellow Pages of a large city phone book.

Dogs—Raise a puppy to be a Canine Companion for Independence. Puppy raisers begin working with pups that are eight weeks old.

You keep them for a year and teach them skills such as stay, sit, come, and an amazing "toilet on command." Call Canine Companions for Independence in your state or visit http://www.caninecompanions.org.

Dog Blood Donors: Check with your local veterinary hospital regarding dog blood transfusions. Veterinarians commonly give blood plasma to dogs with blood clotting problems, severe infections, or anemia, and there is a constant shortage of dog blood. Veterinarian clinics have to pay a lot more per pint of whole dog blood than hospitals have to pay for whole human blood.

Dolls—If you collect dolls, you may want to contact Kit Birmingham, who creates beautiful cornhusk dolls and one-of-a-kind dolls sculpted from polymer clay. She specializes in Santas, Mrs. Santas, and character dolls. Write to her at P.O. Box 2260, Tijeras, NM 87059.

Domestic Violence—Help set up a training program for corporate officials to increase understanding and awareness of domestic violence issues. Work with managers to provide employees concrete suggestions for creating a supportive environment for victims. If you are experiencing abuse or if you are abusing someone, get help for yourself by calling Social Services. Also, for both men and women, there is a 24-hour Domestic Violence Hot Line; call 1-800-799-7233 for help near you. Also, take advantage of the helpful resources at www.ndhv.org.

Donate—
Donate Your Collections or Valuables: Donate these to a museum, school, or library. Make provisions to pay for the collection's

maintenance and growth. Also consider donating property to a worthy cause, organization, or government program. Please be aware that your intentions for the property's use may or may not be carried out.

Donate Musical Instruments: All kinds of musical instruments could be donated to schools, churches, hospitals, nursing homes, and so on. Your generosity may help somebody realize a dream to play music who might never be able to afford the instrument they wish to play. Tricia recently read about a grand piano donated to a hospital and placed in the lobby. It is played by volunteers and walk-ins, professional or amateur, and it brings hours of joy to many people.

Donate Your Organs after Death: Organs you can donate after death are your heart, kidneys, pancreas, lungs, liver, and intestines. Tissues you can donate include eyes, skin, bone, heart valves, veins, and tendons. The donor's family or estate is never charged. For more information about organ donation, call 1-888-894-6361 (www.unos.org) or 1-804-782-4920 (www.shareyourlife.org).

Draw — Draw poker, or draw pictures or cartoons, or draw up wills, depending on your expertise.

Dreams — Is there something that you've always dreamed of doing? Is it possible to fulfill that dream now?

Talk about a dream, try to make it real.

—Bruce Springsteen

Driving — Volunteer to drive for those who cannot drive themselves. Go online to www.pointsoflight.org, the Points of Light Foundation, to see what you can do to help. Also, consider becoming a driver for Meals on Wheels (www.mowaa.org) in your community.

Eating—For a special treat, make a root beer float or a banana split with chocolate sauce, nuts, and maraschino cherry, topped off with a dab of whipped cream.

Eldercare—A great website for both professionals and family members looking for information on eldercare can be found at www.caregiver.org, site of the Family Caregiver Alliance. You could open an eldercare home: A retired journalist, Bill McBean, found a new calling that way. He says, "If you had told me five years ago that I would be changing old people's diapers, I would have said you were whacked. But this has made me feel useful for the first time in my life."

Elderhostel—Through this popular program for adults 55 and over, you can travel to sites throughout the U.S. and over 90 other countries and take classes for a very reasonable fee. You might stay in a college dorm, an inn, a hotel, or a retreat center (Elderhostel takes care of making the accommodations, which vary by location). Call 1-877-426-8056 or visit www.elderhostel.org. Sign up to receive their catalogs of the seasonal and types of programs they offer.

Engage—Engage anybody and everybody in conversation.

Enter—Enter contests of all kinds.

Estate — Have pity on those who will sort through your house and possessions after you're gone. Sort through any junk now and get rid of it yourself. List collections and valuables — you probably don't want your heirs selling your Heisey Orchid stemware or your priceless jade collection, kachina collection, diamonds, or Oriental rugs for pennies at a garage sale. Make your own funeral and burial arrangements.

Estate Planning — Buy a book such as *The Complete Book of Trusts* by Martin M. Shenkman, a tax and estate attorney (John Wiley & Sons). See your attorney about creating a trust, or visit www.legalzoom.com for "lawyer-free pricing."

 Exercise — Start an exercise program, after first consulting your doctor. Regular exercise, whether it be walking, biking, aerobics, swimming, weight training, or other form will give you more energy and a sense of well-being. If you choose an exercise program you enjoy, you'll be more likely to stick to it. Try the Oriental art of tai chi, which is recommended for lowering blood pressure and reducing the risk of falling. Check your library or bookstores for information about tai chi.

If you really want something, you can figure out how to make it happen.

—Cher

Eyeglasses — Collect old eyeglasses in an office building or apartment building near your home by placing a cardboard box in the lobby. When the box is full, contact Medical Ministry International for shipping instructions (the Texas office is P.O. Box 1339, Allen, TX 75013, phone 1-972-727-5864, fax 1-972-727-7810, e-mail mmitx@mmint.org; in Canada call 1-905-524-3544 or e-mail mmican@mmint.org; visit www.mmint.org for more about the Medical

Ministry). Or visit www.uniteforsight.org and follow their plan for an easy way to start an eyeglass drive with Unite For Sight posters.

Fall Colors—Take trips to see the spectacular fall colors, which are very different in different parts of the country.

Family Memory Book—Start a notebook in which you write what and when your grandchildren say something humorous or heart-touching. You can share these items with your loved ones throughout life.

Fast-Draw Contest—Enter a fast-draw contest. They are usually held in historic towns such as Dodge City, Kansas; Deadwood, South Dakota; Laughlin, Nevada; or Lafayette, Colorado. Fast-draw guns shoot .45 caliber blanks to break balloon targets at 5, 8, 10, 12, and 15 feet. They also hit metal impact targets with wax bullets at 5–15 feet. Timing is by digital readout; electronic fast-draw timers score contestants to a thousandth of a second. The world records as of April 1, 2004, for single shot standing blanks 4" @ 8' were 0.219 in the men's division and 0.255 in the women's division. Check out the website www.fastdraw.org/wfda for calendar of events, rules, and world records.

Faux Art—This is a method of painting decorations on walls. Learn how to do it, or have it done.

Feel-Good Books— Read a "feel-good" book. Try Jan Karon's series, The Mitford Years, set in North Carolina. So far six books have been published as mass-market paperbacks (others in the series are available only in trade editions): in order they are *At Home in Mitford* (Penguin), *A Light in the Window* (Penguin), *These High, Green Hills* (Viking), *Out to Canaan* (Penguin), *A New Song* (Penguin), and *In This Mountain* (Penguin). All the books in this beloved series are available as audiocassettes.

Festivals— Attend the festivals in your state. Festivals include all kinds of exhibits and activities. They can be focused on music, art, cowboy poetry, quilts, hang gliding, chocolate, auto races and shows, pioneer days, burro days, hot-air balloons, black arts, ice sculptures, kinetic conveyance sculpture races. . . . You're practically guaranteed to enjoy yourself! Find information about festivals all over the world by visiting www. festivals.com.

Luck is what you have left over after you give 100 percent.

—Langston Coleman

Find a Need— And fill it! If you need something, someone else needs it, too. Start looking at what you use every day, even the smallest items. Ask, "What if . . . ? Why not . . . ? What could be improved upon? What little gizmo do I need? If I had arthritis, could I . . . ? If I were in a wheelchair, could I . . . ?"

Fire Safety— Check throughout your home for fire hazards and make appropriate changes to reduce the chance of fire.

Flooding— Figure out ways to prevent or alleviate flooding. It happens every year with devastating consequences. Should the river beds be dug out? Should higher and stronger dikes be built? Any ideas?

Flower Arranging — Do you have a knack for flower arranging? Florists employ extra help during holidays such as Christmas, Easter, and Mother's Day. Enjoy Web-surfing via www.flowerarranging.com.

Folk Dancing — Teach others any specialized dances you know, for example, Greek, Russian, Indian, or other dances; or teach folk songs. Offer a class, or volunteer to visit a school or other organization to share your folk knowledge. Listings of dances and dance locations across the country can be found at www.folkdancing.org.

Food — Try unusual foods: Moroccan, Algerian, Tunisian, Japanese, Thai, Vietnamese, Ethiopian. Prepare dishes yourself, or visit an ethnic restaurant. Listen to recordings on the safest way to cook, serve, store, and travel with food. Proper food handling tips are found on most food packages. Get advice from an expert live on the USDA Meat and Poultry Hotline at 1-888-MPHotline (674-6854).

Foreign Languages — Learn a foreign language. Maybe you plan to travel, and learning another language would make your trip more enjoyable. Translators are always needed in the medical field, as well as in the business world and in government. Read the book *How to Learn Any Language* by Barry Farber (Carol Publishing). Consider getting a language degree online or teaching language to kids. Visit www. travlang.com/languages for basic vocabulary in over eighty languages (scroll down to the section with all the flags).

Fraud — If you are a victim of fraud against the elderly or of telemarketing fraud, where the caller asks for money or financial information, call the National Consumers League's National Fraud Information Center at 1-800-876-7060 or go to their website at www.fraud.org.

Friends— Friends will take on a whole new meaning. Retirement can be dull with no one else around. If you're the only one at home on your block during the day, you'll have to scout around for a buddy to do things with. Sociability is really necessary now. If you have several buddies, you can help each other with projects. For instance, you help Bob with a brake job on his car, then both of you help Joe cut and split wood for his fireplace, and then both Joe and Bob help you paint your house. Next week, you and your significant other can go to Bob's mountain retreat with his significant other to help paint the decks and stairways, play miniature golf, have a nice dinner, spend the night, and enjoy the mountains. The week after that you can help Joe hang the new chandelier in the dining room of his daughter's house, and then eat the fresh trout you, Joe, and his son-in-law catch in the afternoon. Retirement can be a big round of receiving and returning favors, to the advantage and enjoyment of everyone concerned.

If you have only one smile in you, give it to the people you love. Don't be surly at home, then go out in the street and start grinning "Good Morning" at total strangers.

—Maya Angelou

Games— Play some of the games people used to play: Authors, Scrabble, dominoes, cribbage, checkers, pinochle, jacks, pick-up-sticks. Consider creating new games. Have a few friends over and enjoy a game of bocce ball, ping pong, pool, or croquet.

Gangster-Style, Murder Mystery Dinner Party— Host your own "How to Host a Murder" dinner party with each of your guests acting out a part. (Each game comes in a box, and there are different themes.) You can make this as realistic as you want by sending out invitations and assigning each guest a role to play, complete with people wearing costumes to suit their parts, or the party can be very casual and impromptu. The instructions are easy to follow, and the game is a *lot* of fun. There are a variety of murder mysteries to solve, available wherever games are sold.

Zest is the secret of all beauty. There is no beauty that is attractive without zest.

—Christian Dior

Garage Sales—Garage sales are a great way to make money, have fun, and meet people. Make sure you have plenty of stuff priced in the nickel and dime range. Be willing to dicker on prices. Make waterproof, easy-to-read signs, and post them on busy streets, pointing in the right direction. Open early in the morning, by seven or eight o'clock, depending on your area. If you wait much later to open, you will have missed about two hundred early-bird buyers. At www.garagesale.com, you can list or find garage sales. You might also want to do "estate sales," where you go in and price everything in the house of a deceased or elderly person, sell what you can, give 75 percent of the proceeds to the relatives, and pocket the other 25 percent. Then you haul away whatever is not wanted or sold, FREE.

Gardening—Maybe you've never had time to have a garden because of your job. Now you can indulge in either a small or a large garden, or maybe change some of your landscaping. Organic gardening is really catching on, and people are looking to buy produce that has not been contaminated with pesticides. Ask the County Extension Service to recommend plants and flowers that attract butterflies and hummingbirds; flower and shade plants that will grow in the shade of your mature trees; or ornamental grasses for your yard. If you don't have space for a garden, contact the County Extension Service—they sometimes offer seniors a ten-foot-square plot for gardening. Does becoming a Master Gardener sound appealing? If so, inquire at the Extension Service, a local botanical garden, or a college in your area for more information.

Extra Produce?: Donate your extra produce to the hungry. Contact your place of worship, homes for battered women, rescue missions, or a community food ministry; or contact America's Second Harvest, a nationwide network of food banks, at 1-800-771-2303 or www.secondharvest.org. If you plant long-keeping root vegetables, such as onions, leeks, carrots, potatoes, and parsnips, these make great winter soups.

Gardening Books: *All New Square Foot Gardening* by Mel Bartholomew (Cool Springs Press) and *How to Grow More Vegetables* by John Jeavons (Ten Speed Press) are only two of the many books out there for whatever kind of gardening you're into.

Gardening in Containers: Consider buying a self-watering container system called Living Tapestries, the Fence That Grows (www.livingtapestries.com). It is a set of interconnecting panels that can be planted with everything from petunias to peppers. The growing medium is sphagnum moss, which increases humidity and lessens frost damage.

Garden Tools: Check out Gardener's Supply Company at www.gardeners.com (click on "Shopping") to order online or request a catalog, or call them at 1-888-833-1412. Another fun site is Garden-scape (www.gardenscapetools.com, 1-888-472-3266). For every $10 Gardenscape Pin sold (a pewter watering can lapel pin), they donate $5 to groups working to make gardening accessible to everyone.

More Internet websites for gardeners:

Better Homes and Gardens
www.bhg.com/bhg/gardening

The Biggest Name in Little Gardens
www.windowbox.com

Gardening on the Web
www.gardening.com

The National Gardening Association
www.garden.org

Weather means more when you have a garden. There's nothing like listening to a shower and thinking how it is soaking in around your green beans.

—Marcelene Cox

Garlic—Enter the Great Gilroy Garlic Recipe Contest and Cook-Off. For contest rules and dates, send a self-addressed, stamped envelope to Gilroy Garlic Festival Association, 7473 Monterey Street, Gilroy, CA 95020 (www.gilroygarlicfestival.com, 1-408-842-1625).

Dad taught me everything I know. Unfortunately, he didn't teach me everything he knows.

—Al Unser

Genealogy—Create or expand the record of your family tree. Check your library for books or a Genealogy Department they may have. Most of the information you find needs to be verified by birth, death, or marriage certificates. Places to start on the Internet include www.heritage quest.com; www.familysearch.org; www.usgenweb.org; www. cyndislist.com; and www.ancestry.com. Some of these websites are free and some charge a fee.

Get Out of the House—For a little while every day, leave your residence, if only to walk around the shopping mall, visit with the neighbors, or enjoy a sack lunch at the park. The sociability of other people is important to emotional health.

Gift for Mom — As a special gift for Mom, send $100 to the National Women's Hall of Fame. They have a program called the Book of Lives & Legacies. Mom will be named to the national institution's Wall of Fame: Her name will be inscribed on a plaque and displayed on a wall in the institution in Seneca Falls, New York. A replica of the plaque will be mailed to you. Call 1-315-568-8060 or visit www. greatwomen.org.

"Give Back" — Give back to society what it has given to you. Do you have a talent you could use to help someone reach their potential?

Give Blood — Make an effort to give blood, or volunteer at a blood bank or blood drive in your community. The gift of your blood may save a life or lives.

 Gluten-Free — If you need wheat-free, gluten-free mixes for cooking or baking, contact Ener-G Foods, Inc., P.O. Box 84487, Seattle, WA 98124 (1-800-331-5222, www.ener-g.com). Quinoa Corporation makes a wheat-free, gluten-free pasta. Write to them at P.O. Box 279, Gardena, CA 90248 (1-310-217-8125, www.quinoa.net). The Gluten-Free Pantry, a Connecticut-based mail-order company, sells gluten-free mixes for brownies, pasta, muffins, bagels, breads, and more. Their address is P.O. Box 840, Glastonbury, CT 06033. Their inquiry and customer service number is 1-860-633-3826, and their order number is 1-800-291-8386. Their website is www.glutenfree.com.

Goals — Buy the book *Goals: How to Get Everything You Want — Faster Than You Ever Thought Possible* by Brian Tracy (Berrett-Koehler). Move beyond a vague idea about what you want to be different in your life. Learn to move past internal barriers and low self-esteem, how to decide if a goal is truly what you want or only what someone else wants for you, and finally how to achieve your goal.

Gold Panning/Prospecting—Do you live in an area where gold mining is a part of its history? If so, you'll probably still find people out panning for gold. Consider joining a group that plans regular gold-panning activities. Visit www.icmj.com (go to "Miners Calendar" section) to see what different groups are up to.

Golf—Golf is great fun, as well as great frustration. Join a golf league and play once or twice a week. You'll meet lots of nice people. On the Internet, visit the GolfWeb and PGA Tour website (www.pgatour.com). To improve your game, watch golf videos, which can be obtained from the library. Watch golf tournaments on television. Take lessons from a golf pro at your club. Golf courses are some of the most beautiful places on earth, and you'll be walking on grass you didn't have to mow, water, or trim. (Golf courses are so beautiful because large amounts of pesticides are used in their maintenance, so don't put golf tees or balls in your mouth and don't walk a course barefoot or in sandals. Wash your hands when you get off the course.) Ping golf clubs were made by Karsten Solheim because he didn't like the ready-made golf clubs; build your own golf clubs in your garage—call the Golf Works at 1-800-848-8358, send a fax to 1-800-800-3290, or go to their website at www.golfworks.com.

Good Luck—Show your lucky streak by wearing Lady Luck Jewelry made from dice, dominoes, and mah-jongg tiles. Some of the proceeds are donated to charity. Visit www.LadyLuckJewelry.com.

Graphoanalysis—Learn how to read people's personality and character traits in their handwriting. Contact the International Graphoanalysis

Society, 842 Fifth Avenue, New Kensington, PA 15068; call 1-724-472-9701; fax 1-267-501-1931; or visit www.igas.com.

Greeter — Be a greeter at your local Wal-Mart store.

Grieving — Try not to grieve too much over friends and loved ones who have divorced, moved away, or died. Concentrate on the good times you had together. Always part as friends so that you will have no regrets if you don't meet again. As the Russian poet Pushkin said, "Never say with grief, 'He is no more,' but rather say with thankfulness, 'He was.'"

Grooming — This continues to be important even in retirement. What if someone calls and wants to go to lunch in thirty minutes? You don't want to decline because you look frumpy or disheveled. If no one calls, you call them. Also, you don't have to look or act old or dirty. Keep your hair trimmed and colored, if you like. Your nails and clothing should be neat and clean. An old friend of Tricia's would look down on his soiled shirt and say, "I used to hate dirty old men and darned if I didn't become one." It's not necessary to spend a lot of money on clothes, either. Goodwill thrift stores and consignment shops often have brand-new or near-new items. You just need to look carefully. You can also find nice clothing at garage sales.

The secret of staying young is to live honestly, eat slowly, and lie about your age.

—Lucille Ball

Habitat for Humanity — Volunteer to help build a home with Habitat for Humanity, which is now building "green," which means they use energy-efficient and environmentally friendly construction techniques. Special skills are not required; anyone can help. Call 1-800-HABITAT (422-4828) or visit www.habitat.org.

Hair — Do you have a knack for working with hair? If you do, this can be an idea for a small, part-time business, or you may find doing haircare for people in nursing homes a rewarding experience. Learn how to french-braid hair. Have a computer imaging service show you how you would look with different hair styles.

Harmonica — Learn how to play a harmonica. For a beginner's guide, send a self-addressed, stamped envelope (#10 size) to Hohner, Inc./HSS, 1000 Technology Park Drive, Glen Allen, VA 23059. Discover the history of the harmonica on their website at www.hohnerusa.com.

Harmony — Have you noticed that nobody seems to know how to harmonize anymore? Teach or learn two-, three-, or four-part harmony. Sing for yourself or to entertain others.

 Health Club or YMCA — Consider joining a health club to aid your physical and cardiovascular well-being. It's also another place to meet people.

Health Newsletter — Get the Wellness Letter, an informative newsletter on preventive medicine, written by the University of California at Berkeley. Try a one-year trial subscription. Write UCB Wellness Letter, P.O. Box 420148, Palm Coast, FL 32142; call 1-800-829-9170; or fill out the form at www.berkeleywellness.com.

 Healthy Eating — Eat a diet rich in fruits, vegetables, and low-fat dairy products to reduce your blood pressure, the risk of heart disease, and the likelihood of stroke.

Hearing — Send for the booklet *Communicating with People Who Have a Hearing Loss* from the Alexander Graham Bell Association for the Deaf and Hard of Hearing, 3417 Volta Place NW, Washington, DC 20007 (1-202-337-5220, TTY 1-202-337-5221, www.agbell.org). The organization works with both adults and teens.

Hearing Dogs — Whether you need a hearing dog or you want to train hearing dogs, there are many wonderful places. For instance, check these out: Dogs for the Deaf, in Central Point, OR (www.dogsforthedeaf.org); Fidos for Freedom, in Laurel, MD (www.fidosforfreedom.org); Paws with a Cause, in Wayland, MI (www.pawswithacause.org); and Texas Hearing and Service Dogs, in Austin, TX (www.servicedogs.org).

 Heart Disease — The American Heart Association has a very informative website (www.americanheart.org) for heart disease (1-800-242-8721) as well as for stroke (1-888-478-7653). The site includes topics such as heart-related diseases, healthy lifestyle, children's health, publications, resources, and fundraising.

Imagination is more important than knowledge.

—Albert Einstein

Help Young People to Be Creative—Get them away from the television. Children need to be doers to develop a sense of appreciation of themselves and others. Give them paper, pencils, crayons, paints, or clay, and let their imagination create the lines and mix the colors. If they are interested in music, buy them an instrument and help them stay motivated to practice.

Heritage—Heritage is your family history. Look back and see if there is something from the old country that people in the U.S. might enjoy.

Hiking—Many hundreds of trails exist in our country and beyond. Some of the trails are probably much closer than you realize. Hiking is wonderful exercise, and it allows you to experience parts of the world that only those willing to engage in these excursions will see. Hiking also allows excellent time for reflection. Read *Trailside Guide: Hiking and Backpacking, Revised Edition* by Karen Berger (W.W. Norton). The guide covers planning and preparing for a trip, getting in shape, technique, safety and first-aid tips, and how to have more fun along the way. The book contains color photographs and drawings throughout. Also check out *Backpacker Magazine* as a terrific hiking resource. See "Hiking Information Sources" in Appendix F for further information.

HMO Comparison—Contact the National Committee for Quality Assurance (NCQA) to find out how your HMO (health maintenance organization) compares with others. You can get a detailed report card on most HMOs. For a free report, call 1-888-275-7585 or visit www.ncqa.org.

Hokey — Do the hokey pokey, bunny hop, chicken dance, conga line, or hucklebuck.

Holiday Pageants — Work with others at your place of worship to stage a play depicting an important event or turning point in the history of your religion. An increasingly popular type of pageant creates "living pictures," a series of tableaus formed by actors, including children, posing in different scenes. The house lights are dimmed and the actors re-pose themselves between scenes. Each scene may be accompanied by narration, delivered either by a narrator or by the actors themselves.

Holidays — Relish your favorite holidays more than ever: Valentine's Day, Independence Day, Oktoberfest, Thanksgiving, Hanukkah, Christmas, Kwanzaa, and so on. Share with your family or friends some of the traditional holiday activities your ancestors delighted in. Enjoy baking, sing-alongs, sleigh rides, handmade decorations, and homemade cards, candies, and gifts. Find great ideas for celebrating holidays at www.holidays.net, or find out about holidays and festivals around the world at www.earthcalendar.net.

Home Maintenance — Have your lawn mowed, windows washed, or snow shoveled in a timely fashion.

Hospice — This concept might be a good business opportunity. Father Paul von Lobkowitz, age sixty-four, started the Hospice of St. John in Lakewood, Colorado, with only "ten cents and a can of paint" in 1976. The hospice serves terminally ill patients; the average length of stay is about twelve days. Information about hospice care can be found at www.hospicefoundation.org.

Hot-Air Balloon—Take a hot-air balloon, glider, or skydiving ride for some special occasion. Attend hot-air balloon races or shows. Balloon clubs all over the world can be located through www.hotairballoon.org.

House-Sit—House-sit for friends or others while they go on vacation.

Not a shred of evidence exists in favor of the idea that life is serious.

—Brendan Gill

How Do You View Retirement?—Do you look at retirement as an opportunity to do things you've always wanted to do but never had time for, or as the beginning of the end? Some people go home, twiddle their thumbs, and die within months after retirement. *Don't let this happen to you!* Reread the Introduction and then pick at least two activities to do within the next month. Don't forget to skim the "Let Your Imagination Soar" activities, too, for ideas.

Humor—"Humor greases the skids of life." Enjoy a good laugh every day. Find humor in tense situations. Read books by Bill Cosby, Dave Barry, and Erma Bombeck (yes, even still). The website www.humorsearch.com has 5000 jokes searchable by topic. Touchstar Productions (www.touchstarpro.com) has many videos and tapes, such as *Laughter and the Immune System* or humor for various illnesses as well as a *Humor Toolkit*.

I Remember Mama—Start an "I Remember Mama" brunch to honor elderly women who might be alone on Mother's Day. See www.iremembermama.org, sponsored by Volunteers of America.

Ice Fishing—Go ice fishing and take along a couple of buddies. Explore this idea further at www.icefishingtheoutdoors.com.

Ideas—Ideas are fleeting. Keep a scrap of paper or a notebook handy to jot down your ideas before they're gone. Enjoy a visit to www.globalideasbank.org.

Identify Your Identity—Just what is your identity? Are you Joe(sephine) Blow, Vice President of Marketing of Higgeldy Piggeldy Stores; or Joe(sephine) Blow, Little League coach, watercolorist, formidable chess player, and champion bass fisher? If your entire identity is in the corporate title you once held or in a corporate structure, you might want to open a business; be a consultant; get on the board of a bank, zoo, or fraternal organization; run for political office; or campaign for a political candidate. Consider joining the Service Corps of Retired Executives (SCORE); visit www.score.org or call 1-800-634-0245. Contact the Small Business Administration in your town or check out their website at www.sba.gov.

Immigrants—Especially if you are proficient in a foreign language, you can help immigrants prepare for the citizenship test and interview. For more information, go to www.us-immigration.com, or contact your place of worship or the U.S. Citizenship and Immigration Services listed in the Federal Government section of your phone book.

Improvisation—Enjoy improvisational comedy. Take or teach a class. Visit or perform in a comedy club. At Laughing Matters Improvisation (www.laughingmatters.com) in Atlanta, performers customize comedy shows for companies, from murder mysteries to fake lectures.

Income Tax—Preparing income tax return forms for elderly people might prove an interesting and rewarding service.

Indoors or Outdoors—Where do you enjoy being? You decide, and then pick appropriate activities.

Insurance—Inventory the contents of your home by photographing or videotaping your possessions, and then keep this record of your belongings in a safe-deposit box. You'll be prepared if disaster strikes, and your insurance company will be more inclined to give you a fair settlement. Shop around for the best prices for homeowner's insurance. AARP insurance is reasonable, especially if you insure your home and cars. You can compare insurance quotes from leading insurance agencies at www.insweb.com. Also, check out long-term care insurance for future coverage needs.

Internet for Seniors—Following are several interesting Internet sites specifically intended for seniors.

ElderHope: Check www.elderhope.com. It is a wonderful resource for every aspect of aging and beyond. Topics include death, loss, grief, life review, and a celebration of life, meditations, and musings.

The Resource Directory for Older People: A directory of government agencies and resource centers on aging. Download from the following site address (be advised, the directory runs about 120 pages!).

www.aoa.gov/eldfam/How_To_Find/ResourceDirectory/ resource_directory.asp

SeniorNet: An international community of computer-using seniors. The website is www.seniornet.org. It supports about 240 community learning centers throughout the United States, where people fifty and older can learn about computers. Over a million older adults have mastered their home computers thanks to this not-for-profit organization. Membership is free. SeniorNet offers online courses and tutorials, research, conferences, and technology. This site is "THE best online forum for retirees," said the *Wall Street Journal*. SeniorNet is headquartered at 1171 Homestead Rd., Suite 280, Santa Clara, CA 95050; phone 1-408-615-0699; fax 1-408-615-0928.

Wired Seniors: This supersite at www.wiredseniors.com makes you feel like you are "in a Web of your own." It is a portal designed to serve the needs of people fifty and older. The "Senior Search" portion provides over 5,000 cyberlinks across all sorts of categories from Art & Humanities to Science to Travel Agents.

World War II Web Ring—A "ring" of websites containing stories, information, and links to anything regarding WWII. The site address does *not* use "www": http://A.webring.com/hub?ring=ww2.

Inventions—Invent something, and then visit the Invention Convention at www.inventionconvention.com to find out how to "turn your idea or invention into millions."

Investing—Reevaluate your investments upon retirement. Learn which investments are good for retirees. After all, you've worked all these years to save for your retirement, so make it enjoyable and lasting. Community colleges offer investment courses, and investment companies offer informative seminars. Go to www.smartmoney.com and www.investorguide.com for information.

Irish Dancing—If you enjoy Irish dancing, consider subscribing to *Irish Dancing and Culture* magazine, 110 Schiller St., Suite 206, Elmhurst, IL 60126 (1-630-279-7521; www.irishdancing.com).

Jackie—Organize a Camelot-era party where people come in "White House cocktail attire" and donate a fee for some worthy cause. Have a contest for Jackie look-alikes to serve as hostesses for the party. Ladies who dress Jackie-style (short dress, pearls, and a pillbox hat) get in free. Decorate in red, white, and blue, and have a great time.

Jam—Play with words. For example, *jam*: make jam, get out of a jam, jam session, jammed together, log jam, traffic jam, jamboree, Jamaica, jambalaya, windjammer, James or Jamie, jammies (pajamas), *Pajama Game* (Broadway play), jamb (door or window), jambeau (leg armor), Jamshid (Persian myth), Katz 'n Jammer Kids (comic strip), and so on!

Join a League—Join a league to bowl, play baseball, golf, or whatever. You will have something to look forward to at least one day each week.

Join the Red Hat Society—The Red Hat Society (for women only) is a group started as a result of the founder's having bought a red hat she thought of as dashing, and then a year later reading the poem "Warning" by Jenny Joseph, which depicts an older woman in purple clothing with a red hat. These ladies really know how to have fun and want you to make up for the sobriety of your youth. They have grown from just a few women to many thousands all over the world. They are easy to spot with their purple outfits, red hats, and big smiles.

Ladies fifty and older are Red Hatters. Ladies younger than fifty may become Pink Hatters and wear pink and lavender. No one is too old to join in the fun. Read *The Red Hat Society, Fun and Friendship after Fifty*, by Sue Ellen Cooper (Warner Books) or visit www.redhatsociety.com.

Karaoke — Enjoy singing in a karaoke night spot, or throw your own karaoke parties with supplies from www.karaoke.com.

Kites — Kite flying is an inexpensive family activity, providing endless hours of fun. For more information, contact Into the Wind, 1408 Pearl Street, Boulder, CO 80302 (1-800-541-0314, www.intothewind.com), a company founded by architects George Emmons and Jim Glass in 1980 and now keeping about twenty employees busy. Join in with the kite communities found at www.aka.kite.org and www.kitelife.com.

Knees — *Heal Your Knees: How to Prevent Knee Surgery and What to Do If You Need It* by Robert Klapper (M. Evans and Company). The book discusses major causes of injury; prevention methods; ways to build strength in the muscle groups surrounding the knee joints; specific exercises; and rehabilitation.

K'NEX — It's the name of a construction toy set (colored pieces of plastic that snap together anywhere along the length of the rod) created by Joel Glickman. Buy this for your grandchildren, or tell them to ask Santa for it. K'NEX is available at toy stores nationwide. K'NEX and Legos can be connected together using "Sploids." Go to www.sploids.com.

Kolache — Enjoy this centuries-old, eastern European pastry filled with nuts, fruit, or meat. You will find recipes to make your own at www.recipezaar.com/39387.

Kudos — Recognize someone's achievement, either privately or publicly!

Landscaping — Along the highways through town, the landscaping may start out as grass but always seems to turn to weeds. Come up with a better idea utilizing xeriscape (a science using drought-resistant plants in landscaping, very popular in arid parts of the country). Check with your local extension service for plants that grow well in your area, be it wet or dry. Great ideas abound at www.epa.gov/greenacres and www.landscaping.about.com/homegarden.

Large Sizes — Large-sized goods for men, women, and children can be ordered from Amplestuff catalog. To obtain a catalog, write to P.O. Box 116, Bearsville, NY 12409, or call 1-866-486-1655. Their website is www. amplestuff.com. For clothing, check out www.plus size.com. You can join the National Association to Advance Fat Acceptance — write to P.O. Box 22510, Oakland, CA 94609. Their website is www.naafa.org.

Laser — Raise funds to implement the use of lasers to remove tattoos from kids who no longer wish to belong to a gang. Maybe you're interested in tattoo removal for yourself. For information on tattoo removal, visit www.tattooremoval.org or consult a dermatologist in your area.

The longer I live the more beautiful life becomes.

—Frank Lloyd Wright

Leading Man/Leading Lady — You and your significant other can be the leading man and leading lady in a steamy novel. You simply fill in a few blanks, such as pet names, occupations, physical descriptions, hobbies, favorite music and perfume, etc. Then you pick one of several plot lines, choose mild or wild versions, and presto — your love life was never better. Great fun for an anniversary or birthday. Order your novel online at www.yournovel.com, or call 1-800-444-3356.

Learn How to Live to Be 100 — Live to be 100 years old and beyond. The following book received mostly 5-star ratings at Amazon.com on this topic. *Can We Live 150 Years? Your Body Maintenance Handbook* by Mikhail Tombak (Healthy Life Press).

Legal Services Made Affordable — If you don't already have a will or trust, now would be a good time to take care of this. Statistics show that 70 percent of all Americans do not have a will. Pre-Paid Legal Services, Inc., and subsidiaries make access to legal services very affordable to its members. Legal service plans are available for individuals, families, small businesses, and groups. To contact a representative in your area, check your local Yellow Pages. You can also call 1-800-654-7757 to obtain information on how to become a member. Their website is www.prepaidlegal.com.

Liberate a Younger Person — Become a life or personal coach. Life coaches or personal coaches help younger people cope with the challenges of their lives. There are about 10,000 life coaches who give advice on everything from financial goals to time management to relationships. Contact International Coach Federation at 1-888-423-3131 or www.coachfederation.org; or visit www.coachville.com.

Libraries—A library is a great place to get books, videos, audiotapes, records, CDs, DVDs, and magazines. Look up business information or pictures of just about anything. Maybe you'd like to work or volunteer at the library and help with displays; provide the children's story hour or movie hour, or help children act out stories they have read. If you're interested in locating libraries all over the world, take a look at www.libdex.com.

Long Term Care—If you have an aging parent, partner, or live-alone friend, discuss long term care with them by stressing how planning now will help them retain control over what happens to them later. For example, how important is it to stay in their own home if the time comes when they can no longer care for themselves? How will they prefer to obtain meals if they can no longer cook? Record their answers for future reference, and share the information with other friends or family members so that everyone will know the aging person's preferences to avoid conflicts in carrying them out. Consider purchasing long term care insurance. For information about this type of insurance or to get a quote from major insurers across the nation, go to www.4freequotes.com.

Inside myself is a place where I live all alone, and that's where you renew your springs that never dry up.

—Pearl Buck

Makeover — Have a makeover done or a glamour picture taken. Watch what the stylist does so you can repeat the makeover at home. If you won't be able to see because they take off your glasses, bring a friend with you and then you can practice on each other. Have a head-to-toe makeover — hairdo, face, clothing. Wearing your best colors will improve your appearance and morale. Take a look at *A Beautiful New You: Inspiration and Practical Advice to Transform Your Looks and Your Life — A Total Makeover Without Cosmetic Surgery* by Laura DuPriest (Three Rivers Press).

Mammogram — Retirement-aged women are well-advised to have a yearly mammogram and gynecological exam. If you're about due or overdue, make the appointment now. Click the pink button at www.thebreastcancersite.com to give underprivileged women access to mammograms.

Martin Luther King Jr. Day — Do something special to celebrate the Martin Luther King Jr. holiday. Get more information by contacting the Corporation for National and Community Service, an organization that engages Americans of all ages and backgrounds in service to help strengthen communities, by calling 1-202-606-5000 or visiting their website at www.nationalservice.org.

Massage — Get a body massage. Learn to massage your significant other. Try shiatsu. Get basic information about all three at www.massageresource.com.

Maze—Try finding your way out of a human maze. Mazes are becoming more popular than ever. Some of the best include The Cherry Crest Farm at Ronks, Pennsylvania (www.cherrycrestfarm.com), which is a very old commercial maze. Helpful maze masters might help you head in the right direction. Beggs Family Farm, Sikeston, Missouri (www.beggsfamilyfarm.com), is a maze simulating an escape from Alcatraz. You can make crayon rubbings of the prison's most notorious prisoners. Try the Davis' Mega Maze at Sterling, Massachusetts (www.davismegamaze.com), which is an ever-changing puzzle. There are 10 bridges that might hurtle you into another cornfield. The Thanksgiving Point at Lehi, Utah (www.cornfield maze.com), is a movie-inspired maze. There is also a scavenger hunt option.

Medical Supplies for Homecare—Here's another "find a need and fill it" idea. If you or someone you know is caring for someone at home, medical supplies for providing homecare can be ordered from www.shieldhealthcare.com (cust. serv. 1-800-765-8775), from www. DrLeonards.com (cust. serv. 1-800-455-1918), or from www.shop mash.com (cust. serv. 1-800-768-9182).

Memory feeds imagination.

—Amy Tan

Memory—Everyone age thirty-five and over has memory lapses. You find yourself in the middle of a room wondering where you were headed and why, or you suddenly draw a blank on what you were about to say, or you can't connect a name with a face. Don't fret. You are probably just distracted, or your memory banks are overloaded. Here's a handy trick: To help yourself concentrate on remembering something, write it down in very small handwriting. Please also refer to *Brain Gym*® Activities (Appendix C) as they may enhance your memory.

"Mending Fences"—If mending fences, or making amends, is important to you, try to resolve any continuing differences with family members or friends. The little (or big) walls we build over things—things we sometimes don't even remember—can rob us of a great deal of gladness in life.

Menopause—Discuss with your doctor options for treating your symptoms. Obtain helpful information at NAMS, The North American Menopause Society, 5900 Landerbrook Drive, Suite 195, Mayfield Heights, OH 44124 (1-800-774-5342, www.menopause.org).

Mentor—Serve as a tutor and mentor with Experience Corps, which offers new adventures in service for Americans over fifty-five. They have offices in 14 cities in the U.S. and work to solve serious social problems, beginning with literacy. Contact the national office at 2120 L Street NW, Suite 610, Washington D.C. 20037 (1-202-478-6190, www.experiencecorps.org).

Mental or Scholastic Interests Can Be Pursued—A neighbor of Tricia's holds seventeen United States Patent Office patents. He has never sold anything from them, but he enjoys the mental gymnastics that lead up to applying for and obtaining those patents. It's all he talks about. He has his creative juices going full blast all day every day.

Metric System—Find a way to promote the metric system in the United States. Check out the U.S. Metric Association at http://lamar.colostate.edu/~hillger (note no "www"). For online conversions, check www.sciencemadesimple.com.

Let your light shine. Shine within you so that it can shine on someone else. Let your light shine.

—Oprah Winfrey

When you have a dream, you've got to grab it and never let go.

—Carol Burnett

Miracle Mile — Find out what the area called "the Miracle Mile" has to offer in Los Angeles. One fascinating stop is the La Brea Tar Pits (www.tarpits.org), and there are quite a few other places you may well find of interest along the famed portion of Wilshire Boulevard.

> *Pain comes like the weather, but joy is a choice.*
>
> —Rodney Crowell

Miracles — Read *A Course in Miracles* (Foundation for Inner Peace) or find out more at www.acim.org. Join a study/support group for whatever's bothering you. Ask friends what the concept of miracles means to them.

> *The thing that is really hard, and really amazing, is giving up on being perfect and beginning the work of becoming yourself.*
>
> —Anna Quindlen

Missionary — Become a missionary or consider some other vocation through your place of worship.

Model — Be a model or an actor or extra in movies made locally. Directors and producers are always looking for mature, suave, debonair people.

Model Railroads — Build/buy/sell/trade trains and layouts.

Moles — Have your moles checked, especially if any of the following conditions exist: (1) The mole is asymmetrical or irregularly shaped. (2) The border is jagged or blurry-looking. (3) The color is getting darker or changing. (4) The diameter is more than one-fourth inch. (5) The mole is uneven or elevated. To learn about spotting skin cancer, visit the website recommended by the American Academy of Family Physicians (1-800-274-2237), which is www.family doctor.org. This site also offers helpful facts in categories such as addictions, asthma, diabetes, mental illness, and much, much more.

Motorhome — Get in your motorhome and see the country! You can join the fun, fellowship, and activities of fellow RV'ers (recreational vehicle users). Good Sam Club and Escapees RV Club are motorhome (RV) clubs with wonderful benefits for their members. Benefits and services include discounts on camping fees, emergency road service, auto and RV insurance plans, medical and hospital insurance plans, trip-routing services, mail forwarding services, lost key and lost pet services, American Express travelers checks, and many, many others. For more information contact the clubs:

Escapees RV Club
100 Rainbow Drive
Livingston, TX 77351
   1-888-757-2582
   www.escapees.com

Good Sam Club
P.O. Box 6888
Englewood, CO 80155
   1-800-234-3450
   www.goodsamclub.com

Wally Byam Caravan Club International (WBCCI)
P.O. Box 612
Jackson Center, OH 45334
   1-937-596-5211
   www.wbcci.org

Moving — Moving is a big decision. Do you want to move to a retirement community with underground secured parking, organized activities, swimming pool, golf, and tennis? Do you want assisted living services

or an on-site health care center? Do you want to stay where you are? For lots of moving ideas and advice, visit www.homestore.com/moving.

Multiple Sclerosis—If you or someone you know has multiple sclerosis, and you want outdoor experiences and confidence-building challenges, contact Adventures Within, 1250 S. Ogden Street, Denver, CO 80210 (1-303-744-8813, www. adventureswithin.org), or visit the National Multiple Sclerosis Society website at www.nmss.org.

Music—Music is important to your mental health. Play music you enjoy listening to. Are you sick and tired of "moldy oldies" that remind you of high school? Country music is popular and fairly easy on the nerves. But does it say what you really want to hear? Write a song about how you feel right now; what you're going through right now; what you're happy or sad about. George Weidler, a policeman in Federal Heights, Colorado, writes songs using a tape recorder while in his patrol car. He wrote a tearjerker titled "Who'll Find the Children?" about missing children. He was recognized by Find the Children, a nonprofit organization in Los Angeles, which used Weidler's creation as its theme song.

Music Festivals—Attend music festivals from Mozart to jazz. Contact Gateway Music Festivals and Tours, P.O. Box 1165, Monticello, MN 55362 (1-800-331-8579, www.musicfestivals.com).

E*verybody has difficult years, but a lot of times the difficult years end up being the greatest years of your whole entire life, if you survive them.*

—Brittany Murphy

Needlecrafts — Try knitting, crocheting, embroidery, or needlepoint; all are fun and easy to learn. Visit www.needlecraftshop.com, www. anniesattic.com, www.stitching.com, and www.velona.com.

New York Public Library Telephone Reference Service — These wonderful people can answer almost any question in just a few minutes. They have countless encyclopedias, almanacs, and dictionaries, including volumes on trademarks, inventions, coins, holidays, temperature and heat-wave records, whatever interests you. Call 1-212-340-0849 Monday through Saturday, 9:00 A.M. to 6:00 P.M. (Eastern standard time). You can find similar information on their website, www.nypl.org.

Newseum — Visit the Newseum, a multimedia monument to the world of news. They are relocating from the original site in Arlington, Virginia, to Washington, DC, and will be completed in 2007. You can check what the news of the day was on the day you were born. Their website at www.newseum.org will take you on an online tour of some of their exhibits, from the fall of the Berlin Wall to how the media played a part in the space race to the moon. If you have an artifact you would like to donate, or if you are interested in being a volunteer, their toll-free number is 1-888-NEWSEUM (639-7386).

Newspaper — Read the newspaper for ideas of things to do, buy, or sell. Do the crossword, sudoku, and other puzzles. Read the funnies.

Nursing Home Pets—Contact your local Humane Society and ask about taking dogs and kittens into nursing homes to boost residents' morale during visits. Read *Life Worth Living* by Dr. William Thomas, an award-winning book about a program called the Eden Alternative, which uses animals, plants, and children to fight the plagues of loneliness, helplessness, and boredom in elderly persons (VanderWyk & Burnham).

Open Houses—Hold an open house for any special occasion. Go to realtors' open houses and see how other homes are decorated.

Orienteering—Learn to use a compass to find your way around. Read *Land Navigation Handbook: The Sierra Club Guide to Map, Compass & GPS, Second Edition* by W. S. Kals and Clyde Soles (Sierra Club Books). Orienteering classes are sometimes available at local outdoor sporting goods stores, such as REI (1-800-426-4840, www.rei.com). Go to the United States Orienteering Foundation website at www.us.orienteering.org to find out more about this fun and challenging sport with local clubs all over the country.

Osteoporosis—Fight osteoporosis through exercise, such as walking, dancing, and weight training. Get your doctor's advice before starting the exercise program. If you are taking Fosamax, take it with *warm* water. Learn what you can do to prevent osteoporosis by visiting www.nof.org.

Pain—See your doctor. Consider hypnosis, acupuncture, massage therapy, herbal therapy, or other alternative medicine. Contact the American Pain Society at 1-847-375-4715 or go to www.ampainsoc.org. You might also find help at www.partnersagainstpain.com.

Paint and Brighten Up Your Home with Color—A fresh coat of paint and some colorful accessories will do wonders for your home.

> Life is a great big canvas and you should throw all the paint on it you can.
>
> —Danny Kaye

Paint Stick—Try the Paint Stick. The handle is a hollow tube with a plunger that sucks up about a pint of paint directly from the can and delivers it to the wall through a perforated roller. It gives a more even finish and saves time. Made by HomeRight, order the Paint Stick by calling 1-800-264-5442.

Painting—Learn to paint with oils, acrylics, or water colors. Barb's mom hadn't drawn or painted (other than household painting) since she was a child in school. In her late forties, she took an art class at a community college and has been hooked ever since. She discovered a hidden talent, and her paintings are truly beautiful (says her objective daughter!). This is one example of how someone's life can be changed through a new hobby, and she has made many new friends along the way. Some artists she knows have had their paintings printed as greeting cards.

> Appealing workplaces are to be avoided. One wants a room with no view, so imagination can meet memory in the dark.
>
> —Annie Dillard

Peace and Quiet—Peace and quiet are necessary while you're trying to think of something new. Turn off the television or radio. Just be quiet and let yourself think. Be by yourself periodically. Let your creative juices flow. If you have a lot of noise and confusion in your life, snatch a moment now and then for your project. Go for a walk without the earphones. Keep a note pad with you at all times to jot down your ideas. Pinpoint what you want to think of. Then forget about it. In the middle of the night when it's quiet and you have the time, answers will come to you. Get out of bed and write down your thoughts. Don't think to yourself, "That's a good idea. I'll remember it for morning." Unfortunately, in the morning you won't remember anything except that you had a great idea. Get up and write down the gist of your idea. Much of this book was drafted in this manner—in the middle of the night.

Peanut Butter Cookies—This recipe for peanut butter cookies is unique in that there is no flour in it. For those who suffer from celiac disorder, recipes that don't contain flour are a real treat. (See the entry "Gluten-Free" for more information on gluten-free food.)

12-ounce jar of peanut butter (We think Jif has the best flavor.)

1 cup sugar
1 teaspoon vanilla
2 egg whites beaten stiff

Combine peanut butter, sugar, and vanilla; mix well. Fold in beaten egg whites. Roll dough into small balls and place on an ungreased cookie sheet. Use a fork to flatten each ball into a cookie form. Bake at 375 degrees for 8 minutes.

People Sixty and Older — Market something to people sixty and older, or write something for or about them. This age group controls the majority of all financial assets in the U.S. and more than half of all discretionary income. In 2006, when the oldest of the Baby Boomers turned sixty, someone was turning sixty about every five seconds. What does this group like? What don't they like? What do they need? What will they need? In the case of the Baby Boomers and the Generation-Xers, how did you cope or live at their ages of thirty, forty, fifty, or sixty?

Pets — If you don't have a pet, think about getting one. Pets can be wonderful companions that give you lots of warm, fuzzy feelings. They do need a lot of love, care, and attention, so be sure having a pet will fit in with your lifestyle. If you can't own a pet, volunteer at an animal shelter.

Pet-Sitting: It's very hard for people to leave their pets with just anybody while they're away. Pet-sitting is a service you can provide either in your home (be aware of your city's ordinances regarding animals) or at the owners' homes. Check with other pet boarding services to determine what you can charge for these services in your area. You'll have no problem getting repeat business and referrals.

Purina Pets for People: Local humane organizations give pets to people who are sixty years and over at little or no cost. Purina pays for most fees just to save homeless pets and give them to people who will enjoy them. Kudos to Purina, who implemented a matching gifts program and provided 150 tons of food to hurricane areas in 2005.

Sick Pets: Round-the-clock consultation is offered by the ASPCA Animal Poison Control Center, allied with the University of Illinois College of Veterinary medicine. Call them at 1-888-426-4435. There is a small fee per case.

Photo Albums — When you organize your photos in albums, add the names of places and people, and dates where applicable. If you have trouble remembering information about a snapshot, go ahead and put it in the album anyway. When you're sharing your photo albums with family and friends, somebody else may remember what you don't, and then you can add the information.

Photography — Take pictures of places you visit and people you see. Put together a photo album to keep your photos organized. Take a photography course and develop your creative photography skills. Some of your pictures could be enlarged and made into unique gifts for family and friends. Have your portrait taken, or that of the whole family.

Picnic — Enjoy a picnic in the park. You can do this with a friend, with children, or by yourself. Take a book to read or a game to play. You'll be sure to relax and enjoy yourself!

Places to Retire — Read the book *What You Need to Know to Plan the Retirement You Deserve, Sixth Edition* by David Savageau (Wiley). Also check www.money.com/retire.

Plants—Learn about edible and medicinal plants. Grow, buy, sell, and trade plants of all kinds. Offer to maintain plants in a community building or public space.

Plays—Attend plays and performances put on by your local high schools and colleges.

Poetry—Do you enjoy reading poetry or writing poetry? Keep your eyes and ears open for poetry gatherings both far and near.

Examples of Gatherings: The Colorado Cowboy Poetry Gathering occurs in January during the annual stock show in Denver, Colorado. This event was fashioned after The Gathering in Elko, Nevada, which was started more than a decade ago and is known worldwide. These gatherings offer lots of rhyme from men and women who work the land; authentic Western music; plenty of humor; and real cowboy food. For a list of cowboy poetry events all over the country, visit www.cowboypoetry.com. Shadow Poetry (www.shadowpoetry.com), 1209 Milwaukee St., Excelsior Springs, MO 64024 (fax 1-208-977-9114) was created as a place for writers to walk "out of the shadows" with their poetry.

Real happiness comes from inside. Nobody can give it to you.

—Sharon Stone

Poetry Contests: Enter one through the International Library of Poetry, 1 Poetry Place, Owings Mills, MD 21117 (1-410-356-2000). This contest is open to everyone and entry is free. Send in only one original poem, any subject, any style, no longer than twenty lines, with your name and address at the top of the page. You can also enter the contest online at www.poetry.com. They provide information and techniques to help with writing poetry.

Poisons—Be careful with the following home products, which can be dangerous if swallowed or, in some cases, touched. Many cause severe damage to eyes. Some should be used only with proper ventilation, as they are dangerous to breathe. Be sure all products listed on the following page are kept out of reach of children. Keep containers clearly labeled and properly stored. Discard expired products. The number for Poison Control is 1-800-222-1222. Post it near your telephone.

Potentially dangerous home products:
> alcohol (rubbing and liquor)
> antidepressant and heart medications
> antifreeze, brake fluids, solvents
> cleaning products
> furniture polish
> iron supplements
> lamp oil
> paint thinner and petroleum products
> perfumes
> pesticides
> tobacco products of all kinds

Police — Volunteer to work for the police department. Take a police academy course for civilians, if one is available to you. It's an interesting experience.

Privacy — For a free *Consumer Action Handbook* that includes information about protecting your privacy and similar valuable topics, call the Federal Citizen Information Center at 1-888-8PUEBLO (878-3256) or visit their website at www.consumeraction.gov.

 PSA Test — Men should have a PSA (prostate-specific antigen) screening test done regularly. For more facts, write to the Prostate Cancer Foundation, 1250 Fourth Street, Santa Monica, CA 90401, call 1-800-757-CURE (2873), or visit www.prostatecancerfoundation.org. Eating a diet rich in fruits and vegetables and low in red meat may reduce your risk of prostate cancer.

Pumpkin—Enter a pumpkin growing or a pumpkin decorating contest.

Quebec—Study the history and culture of Quebec. Plan and enjoy a trip there. Pick other cities or regions of interest to you.

Quilting—An art derived from necessity many years ago, quilting has become popular again in recent years. Quilting techniques are now used to make beautiful wall hangings and delightful articles of clothing. Classes and information are offered through fabric stores, colleges, public television stations; many areas also have quilting groups. Consult your local Yellow Pages under *Quilting* for stores that specialize in quilting. Order kits and supplies at Hearthside Quilts, P.O. Box 610, 90 Mechanicsville Road, Hinesburg, VT 05461. Their phone number is 1-800-451-3533, and their website is www.nvo. com/hearthside.

Quire, Quoin, Quotidian—Look up words you don't recognize. Buy a Scrabble dictionary and challenge someone to an exciting game. Stimulate your brain this way.

Quit Smoking—If you're still smoking after all the public health information you've heard and read, it's time to quit. You may lengthen your life. Bones get more fragile as we age, and that is why older people are more prone to fractures. Smoking inhibits the regeneration of new bone in fractures. Try acupuncture to help you quit. Visit the Quit Smoking QuitNet at www.quitnet.org. See American Lung Association in Appendix G.

Races—You don't need to place a bet to enjoy being at the races. Attend greyhound races, the wiener dog nationals, frog races, horse races, car races, drag races, or motocross.

Radio —Try radio-controlled or battery-operated cars, boats, and planes. Are you interested in ham radio? Here is a useful website to know about: www.qth.com/#ham. Also look for magazines in local bookstores or at newsstands.

Reading—How many of us love to read but have had very little time to do so? Now's your chance to catch up on those mystery, science fiction, old western, romance novels, and bestsellers you've been wishing you had time to curl up with. Go to a book signing and meet the author. Some places allow you to register to curl up in a chair in a bookstore window and read for an hour.

Real Estate—Buy, sell, trade, fix up, or rent real estate. Study for your realtor's license.

Recall a Storm — Recall a crippling blizzard, storm, or tornado in your town, and write a story about it. Submit it to the local paper.

Recipes — Put together a book or booklet of some of your family's favorite recipes. Have copies made for family members or anyone you choose.

Reconcile — To help yourself repair relationships, read *The Solo Partner: Repairing Your Relationship on Your Own, Second Edition* by Phil DeLuca (Alexander). Read *Do It Yourself Relationship Repair Guide* by Nan Einarson (Authorhouse). You can also visit www.relationship saver.com.

Recreation — Check into a compilation of hunting, fishing, and hiking opportunities offered by the federal land agencies (National Park Service, Bureau of Land Management, Bureau of Reclamation, U.S. Army Corps of Engineers, Federal Highway Administration, U.S. Fish and Wildlife Service, Tennessee Valley Authority, and others). You can search by state in about twenty categories (e.g., camping, lodging, water sports) at www.recreation.gov.

Recycle — It's being done everywhere. Maybe you can figure out a way to use or manufacture recycled materials. The American Plastics Council has an informative website on the roles of plastic in the home, sports safety and performance, the garden, the automotive and medical fields, and green-building for a sustainable environment (www.americanplasticscouncil.org, 1-800-243-5790).

P*artake of some of life's sweet pleasures. And yes, get comfortable with yourself.*

—Oprah Winfrey

Reflexology — Have your feet massaged at a reflexology clinic. Treating your feet will work wonders for your whole body. Find reflexology-related sites at www.reflexology.org and www.reflexology-usa.org.

Refurbish — Do you enjoy refurbishing things like cars, furniture, or even houses? Refurbishing can be a hobby or an idea for a small business.

 Relax — Learn to relax. This may take a while. You don't have to punch a time clock or account for every minute. The only time you need to set the alarm clock is to make an early tee time, to go motorcycling, or to play tennis. It's all right to take a leisurely stroll, have a nap after lunch, and visit with the neighbors. To help you relax, lift your eyebrows toward the ceiling; drop your jaw toward the floor. Then drop your shoulders toward the floor and move your elbows out away from your body. Check for books or tapes at the library that can provide helpful information on relaxation. You may also want to try yoga or tai chi.

Remarriage — A new marriage can be wonderfully exciting, but be aware of the risks. The woman, for instance, may lose her deceased husband's pension. Check with Social Security or other pension plan provider. You may want to consider premarital agreements.

Rendezvous — Attend a Mountain Man or Muzzleloader Rendezvous or a Native American Powwow, festivals recreating the West's earlier days. Participants dress in period costumes and reenact activities from Revolutionary times onward. Find products and event calendars at www.crazycrow.com (1-800-786-6210). Also visit the National Muzzle Loading Rifle Association website at www.nmlra.org (1-800-745-1493).

Rental Property — Clean up your rental property. Slum property or poorly maintained property is becoming an increasing problem all over the country. As an example, Phoenix and other Arizona cities are taking an active role in fighting it. In Phoenix the Slumlord Task Force names a "Dirty Dozen" slum list using objective criteria, including number of police calls, and city and county code violations on the properties.

Retire — Retire where it's cheaper to live, where your support system is, where your family is, or where the neighborhood caters to seniors.

Retired Friends — You need friends who are also retired. When people are first married, they suddenly don't have as much in common with their single friends. It's like that for you now. You won't have as much in common with working friends.

Accept what people offer. Drink their milkshakes. Take their love.

—Wally Lamb

Retirement Fund — Will Social Security be bankrupt by the year 2040? You will definitely need your own savings, stocks, annuities, or bonds.

If you obey all the rules, you miss all the fun.

—Katharine Hepburn

Romance — Enhance your romance with a FantaSuite experience. You'll find suite themes from Caesar's Court and Sherwood Forest to the futuristic Space Odyssey. Robes, chocolates, flowers, and baskets are available at some locations. Following (on next page) is a listing of locations and their phone numbers. Be sure to call for a picturesque brochure of the suite themes being offered, or visit www.fantasuite.com for an insider's view of the rooms. Gift certificates are also available.

Greenwood Inn & FantaSuite Hotel
Greenwood, Indiana
1-800-444-7829

Ramada Limited
Burnsville, Minnesota
1-800-666-7829

Don Q Inn
Dodgeville, Wisconsin
1-800-666-7848

Roosevelt Memorial—Visit the 7.5-acre Franklin Delano Roosevelt Memorial on the Mall in Washington, DC. For more details, visit www.nps.gov/fdrm.

Run Errands—Provide courier service for lawyers or real estate offices. Some couriers go by bicycle or rollerblades and some by automobile. Take your pick.

Running—Run in a 5- or 10-km race for a special event. Train with *Runner's World, the Cutting-Edge Runner* by Matt Fitzgerald (Rodale).

Safety in Your Car—To deter criminals, buy a mask, stuff it with rags, fasten the mask on top of a pillow, put a man's jacket around the pillow and a man's hat on top of the mask, prop the dummy up in the front seat, and you'll have what looks like a passenger riding with you. There's safety in company.

Never let a fool kiss you, or a kiss fool you.

—Joey Adams

Save Money on Greeting Cards—Write your friends a silly poem. Print it by hand or on your computer on plain or parchment paper. With the help of a rhyming dictionary and a little time, you can come up with a personalized greeting they'll love.

Save Money on Haircuts—Learn to cut your own hair and family members' hair. Do it yourself three or four times and then have a salon or barber shop cut it the next time. After a little practice, you may find your haircuts aren't so bad.

Say No!—Say no to people who want to waste your time. If you're not interested, just say no!

And then, not expecting it, you become middle-aged and anonymous. No one notices you. You achieve a wonderful freedom. It is a positive thing. You can move about, unnoticed and invisible.

—Doris Lessing

Scams—Seniors should be aware of scam strategies and ways to protect themselves from scams. Be very cautious of door-to-door and telephone solicitations. You have a right to cancel a purchase made over the phone or by door-to-door solicitation up to three days from the date of purchase. Beware of seminars or workshops that are advertised by flyers left in the mailbox or on your doorstep. Be very cautious about signing documents without getting an attorney's advice. Be alert for e-mail scams, of which there are many kinds! Subscribe (free) to Internet ScamBusters at www.scambusters.org.

School—Go back to school! Take classes, or get another degree. Maybe you're interested in the arts, photography, the history of other countries, astronomy, crafts, or almost anything else. Goodness only knows what adventures and experiences can evolve from going back to school.

Science—Go online and explore the Boston Museum of Science website at www.mos.org. Get your daily science "fix" at www.science daily.com or visit the AAAS website at www.sciencemag.org.

Science Books for Children—Enjoy learning about science with your favorite children. There are books out to help make the experience pleasurable and memorable. The Janice VanCleave series offers a great variety; one appropriate for children ages 9–12 is titled *Janice VanCleave's Teaching the Fun of Science* (Jossey-Bass). Buy books in the Magic School Bus series by Joanna Cole and Bruce Degen (Scholastic) for younger children. The series is available in books, videos, DVD, and as videogames. Visit www.scholastic.com/magicschoolbus to get a more interactive look at the books. Also check out *190 Ready-to-Use Activities That Make Science Fun* by George Watson (Jossey-Bass). We wish these books were around to help make science more interesting when we were kids!

T*o find fulfillment . . . don't exist with life—embrace it.*
—Jim Beggs

Scrapbook—Go through those old shoeboxes of treasures from past parties, trips, plays, and life experiences, and put them into a scrapbook. To find the supplies you will need to make your scrapbook exciting, call Times to Cherish at 1-800-848-2848 or go to their website at www.timestocherish.com.

Sea—Are you drawn to life on the sea, or in the sea? Do you enjoy sailing, deep sea fishing, snorkeling, or scuba diving? Do you want to live by the sea? Would you be interested in underwater photography? Coral or abalone harvesting? Hunting for sunken treasure or ships?

Seasonal Contests—Start seasonal contests for guessing when the first measurable snowfall will occur; when the first robin or crocus will appear; when fall color will be at its peak, etc.

Sell—If you're interested in network marketing, sell Amway, Avon, Fuller Brush, Nu Skin, Shaklee, Stanley Home Products, Tupperware, or products for another company. If you want to sell your home, buy the book *How to Sell Your Own Home* by William F. Supple, Jr. (Picket Fence Publishing). You may also want to take a look at the National For Sale By Owner Association website found at www.nfsboa.com.

Senior Centers—They're full of activities with arts and crafts, bridge, dancing, day trips and excursions, and health and exercise equipment.

Aging is not "lost youth" but a new stage of opportunity and strength.

—Betty Friedan

Senior Discounts and Bargains—Ask for senior discounts. You won't get them if you don't ask. Airline tickets and hotel rooms may be discounted (see also Appendix F). Restaurants often offer senior discounts, and so do retail stores such as Montgomery Ward, Sears, auto stores, and golf shops. Contact a large local bank for possible senior travel clubs. Many have them. Just ask. Request furniture discounts and catalogs by calling Cherry Hill Furniture at 1-800-328-0933 and visiting www.wholesalewall coverings.com. For drugs by mail, a company that has very favorable pricing is Family Meds at 1-888-787-2800 (www.familymeds.com).

Senior Resorts — Plan to vacation at retirement community destinations where mature travelers can obtain inexpensive rental units that make resort vacationing affordable. Usually only one person in the couple must be fifty-five or older; you have to spend some time touring the property and listening to a sales pitch.

Northwest Arkansas: Here you will find a gentle climate, a low cost of living, and good housing. Arkansas has a large percentage of retirees. Newcomers are lured by parklike retirement communities for people with active lifestyles. Bella Vista Village is one of the largest retirement communities in the Ozarks. More than 8,000 homes are tucked into this rolling 36,000+ acre preserve about 30 miles north of Fayetteville near the Missouri border. There are 8 golf courses and 8 lakes. At Bella Vista Village, visitors get guest cards for low-cost golf. To schedule a get-acquainted visit, contact Bella Vista Village, 2 Riordan Road, Bella Vista, AR 72714 (1-800-553-6687). For that and similar communities, visit www.cooper-homes.com.

Sun Cities in the Southwest (www.suncities.com): Stay in furnished homes in Palm Springs (1-800-533-5932); in Tucson (1-800-422-8483); near Phoenix (1-800-528-2604); and near Las Vegas (1-800-987-9875).

Tampa Bay, Florida: You can spend up to a week in Sun City Center, a retirement community twenty miles south of Tampa that is home to about 13,000 senior citizens. Contact Sun City Center, P.O. Box 5698, Sun City Center, FL 33571 or call 1-800-924-2290.

Sewing—Do you enjoy sewing? Do you know how to sew? There are many different types of sewing to fill in a few of those retirement hours/days. Maybe you enjoy making alterations (which can be a small business for you), making window treatments, working with upholstery, sewing crafts, designing clothes, or making patterns. Maybe you have an idea that involves sewing and would fill a special niche—for example, you might create clothing for people with special medical needs or disabilities. Barb read of a woman who created custom-fitted bedding sheets for boat owners, and another woman who designed clothes that were works of art. The possibilities are as extensive as your imagination. Another idea is to sew all night at one of the enterprising sewing machine companies that host all-night sewing marathons every year. You bring in your machine and whatever you want to work on, and share munchies with other people there.

> Most women set out to try to change a man, and when they have changed him, they don't like him.
>
> —Marlene Dietrich

Sex—Sex may be more enjoyable, leisurely, and creative with more time available. Read *Sex and the Perfect Lover: Tao, Tantra, and the Kama Sutra* by Mabel Iam (Atria).

Share—Share any special talent, skill, folklore, or knowledge. Form a group and teach your specialty to others. Share your magazines and investment and medical newsletters with others.

> The moment of victory is much too short to live for that and nothing else.
>
> —Martina Navratilova

Shopping—Do you absolutely love to shop? Would you be interested in running a service business of shopping for people who are too busy or unable to shop? You could do their grocery shopping, or their shopping for gifts, household items, and so on. You work within their budget, use their money, and charge them a fee for your time (and imagination).

Sign Language—Learn American Sign Language, or teach it to others. For further information, go to www.handspeak.com or go to www. signlanguage.org.

Silence—Go somewhere to enjoy silence for a weekend. Try a convent, an abbey, an ashram, or a retreat. Perhaps your local library has a copy of *Sanctuaries: The Complete United States—A Guide to Lodgings in Monasteries, Abbeys, and Retreats* by Jack Kelly and Marcia Kelly (Harmony/Bell Tower).

I *merely took the energy it takes to pout and wrote some blues.*

—Duke Ellington

Sing-Alongs—They're fun at the piano or organ. Have copies of the words handy and invite a good piano player.

Sister Cities Program—This program pairs towns in the United States with towns in foreign countries. The arrangement provides opportunities for educational, cultural, and technical interchanges. Students and teachers visit their sister city schools, fire and police departments, and town offices and then exchange ideas. Citizens can often arrange vacation visits or house swaps. The program has a waiting list of cities wanting to pair up. For details, go to www.sister-cities.org or call 1-202-347-8630.

 Skiing—You'll have more time to enjoy snow- or water-skiing. If you don't ski already, it's never too late to take lessons! After your seventieth birthday, you may ski free at Winter Park, Colorado.

 Sleep—Get a better night's sleep. You may want to try an air bed made by Innomax. Call 1-800-466-6629. Cuddle Ewe sells an all-wool mattress cover that can be fluffed up, turned over, and taken out and aired. Visit their website at www.cuddleewe.com or call 1-800-290-9199. The National Sleep Foundation offers a free pamphlet called *When You Can't Sleep: ABC's of ZZZ's*. Write to 1522 K Street NW, Suite 500, Washington, DC 20005, or call 1-202-347-3471. That and many more documents are downloadable from their website at www.sleepfoundation.org. The site also has good information regarding sleep and aging.

Sleigh Ride—Take a sleigh ride in a winter wonderland, or a hay ride any time of year. What a romantic idea!

Slow Food Movement—Join an international group out of Italy specializing in leisurely eating. In the U.S., write to Slow Food Movement, 20 Jay Street, #313, Brooklyn, NY 10013 (1-718-260-8000). The website address is www.slow-food.com.

Smile—If you meet someone without a smile, give him one of yours.

A smile is a curve that sets everything straight.

—Phyllis Diller

Spend — Spend some money on yourself. You deserve it!

Spirituality — Your spiritual side may be of special interest at this stage in your life. Attend your place of worship. Make peace with your God. Attend or teach religious education classes. Participate in social groups at your place of worship.

 Sports — Take up one of these popular participatory sports: swimming, exercise walking, or bike riding. Among the most popular spectator sports are car racing, horse racing, professional baseball, and college basketball.

Sports Vision Training — Check out sports vision training to help your golf, tennis, baseball, or volleyball game. For the name of a sports vision specialist in your town, call the American Optometric Association at 1-800-365-2219 (www.aoa.org).

Start Your Own Business — This can provide you with some "mad" money, or you can launch a whole new career. You decide! Are you an entrepreneur? Have you ever dreamed of owning your own business? You're never too old. An entrepreneur's most important qualifications are strong organizational skills, good business sense, some financial sophistication, and a willingness to work hard. You can start your own business, buy an existing business, or buy a franchise and receive guidance from those who know what it takes to make a business successful. The book you are reading right now contains some business ideas, and Appendix D provides some information on starting your own business. Most libraries offer literature full of advice on starting a business, choosing a business to start, bookkeeping for your business, obtaining legal advice, and so on. Community colleges

As long as you're going to think anyway, think big.

—Donald Trump

almost always offer classes to help you with your small business. You may also want to read *Homemade Money: Bringing in the Bucks! A Business Management and Marketing Bible for Home-Business Owners, Self-Employed Individuals, and Web Entrepreneurs Working from Home Base* by Barbara Brabec (M. Evans and Company).

State Parks—State parks welcome volunteers. Consider helping out with tours, trail maintenance, story telling, or in the gift shop. Enjoy the beautiful scenery and working with the public!

Statue Repair and Cleaning—Do you know how to clean and repair crumbling concrete statues? Do a beautifying project around your town.

Stickball—Teach kids the game of stickball using a broom handle and a rubber ball. No uniforms or special training are needed.

Stock Review—Stocks, bonds, mutual funds, and investments of all kinds need periodic review. Make an appointment with your financial advisor to do this if you are an investor.

Storybooks—Make cassette recordings of yourself animatedly reading favorite children's stories. Send the books and tapes to grandchildren, nieces, and nephews. Maybe they will request subsequent titles.

Stress—Control stress. Read the book *Undoing Perpetual Stress: The Missing Connection Between Depression, Anxiety, and 21st Century Illness* by Richard O'Connor, PhD (Berkley Hardcover). Visit www.stress.org.

Study Cartooning—Contact a community college, library, art institute, or bookstore to inquire about classes in cartooning. Take a look at www.tooning.com.

Sunday Brunch—Go out to Sunday brunch. Consider taking your extended family to brunch once a year.

Sweepstakes Scams—If you're the victim of a sweepstakes scam, contact the Postal Inspection Service by writing to Criminal Investigations Service Center, Attn: Mail Fraud, 222 S. Riverside Plaza, Ste. 1250, Chicago, IL 60606, which tips off the post office in cases involving U.S. Mail services. Also notify your state attorney general's office, FTC (Federal Trade Commission), FBI (Federal Bureau of Investigation), and BBB (Better Business Bureau). To check the legitimacy of a sweepstakes before entering, contact the BBB or state attorney general's office.

Tai Chi—Learn tai chi, a uniquely relaxing, invigorating, dancelike exercise. Gentle physical movements help to connect and lubricate the joints while cultivating chi energy throughout the body. Check your bookstore, library, or continuing education program for information on tai chi. Martial arts studios often offer classes. Order tapes, books, supplies, and gear through www.taichi.com.

Taxes — Consult an expert to help you save money on taxes or to set up trusts to protect your money.

Teach — You probably have valuable knowledge and experiences that can be passed on to others, whatever your area of expertise: religion, education, business, athletics, or other area. If teaching appeals to you, particularly as part-time work, check with community colleges, your place of worship, and community groups of interest to you. Maybe you have a hobby you've enjoyed for years and would like to share with others. Teach kids in scout groups and other organizations some of the games you played as a child. You'll get back as much as you give.

> **Y**ou can get everything in life you want if you will just help enough other people get what they want.
>
> —Zig Ziglar

Teachers International — Teach in a foreign country for two or more years. Contact International Schools Services, 15 Roszel Road, P.O. Box 5910, Princeton, NJ 08543 (1-609-452-0990, www.iss.edu). They establish and operate schools, place teachers and administrators, and purchase and ship curricular materials and school supplies. They also publish a quarterly newsletter titled *NewsLinks*. The fall and winter issues advertise upcoming vacancies at schools, invaluable to those seeking educational careers overseas. Another organization of this type is University of Northern Iowa Academic Advising and Career Services, 242 Gilchrist Hall, Cedar Falls, IA, 50614. Their phone number is 1-319-273-2083, and their website is www.uni.edu/placemnt/overseas.

 Teeth — If you have dentures, wear them for three reasons: (1) Not wearing dentures can cause the gums to change and then the dentures won't fit properly; (2) the face looks much better with teeth; and (3) gradual hearing loss can result from not wearing your dentures. If you are not wearing your dentures because they fit improperly, find a dentist who will work to get a proper fit. Brighten your smile with the Rembrandt Dazzling White at-home bleaching system, Rembrandt 2 Hour White, Crest Whitestrips, or other brands, which bleach your teeth (not caps) several shades whiter. A million-dollar smile is hard to beat. See your dentist for a professional consultation. Laser tooth whitening is also available now.

Tetanus Shot—Get a tetanus booster shot. Tetanus can result from even a minor wound or scratch. Most tetanus infections occur in people over the age of sixty, as this age group is the least likely to be immunized.

Theater—Attend a melodrama. Go to plays. Join a theater group and act; be an understudy; work on set decorations or costumes; be a go-fer or a promoter.

Theme Cruises—These are popular because they provide passengers with both an ideal vacation and the opportunity to indulge in a special interest. Try a cruise themed on jazz, gardening, world affairs, sports, fitness, nutrition, big band music, bridge, country music, murder mystery, photography, or routes of the great explorers. For further information on itineraries, travel dates, and prices, contact a travel agent, or call the cruise line directly (see Appendix F).

Spring is nature's way of saying, "Let's party!"

—Robin Williams

Theme Parties— Throw a theme party complete with set decorations. Themes could include Caribbean Cruise, Phantom of the Opera, and many other possibilities. In the Denver area, you would contact Greg or Chris Reinke at 1-303-795-5006. At Halloween they host the Haunted Mansion at 5663 S. Prince Street in downtown Littleton, Colorado. They also have thousands of costumes, masks, gifts, makeup, and accessories for sale or rent. The Reinke Brothers are able to produce parties throughout the country (www.reinke brothers.com).

This Is Your Life— Make a "This Is Your Life" video for yourself or for the birthday or anniversary of someone you love. Equipment you will need includes one TV, one video camera, two VCRs (VCR #1 is to record from, and VCR #2 has a blank tape on which to record to), one editor, and one video enhancer/stereo/audio mixer. (A growing number of camcorders have built-in DVD recorders instead of tape mechanisms. These directions assume use with tape, however.) This equipment is available at electronics/stereo companies such as Soundtrack and Radio Shack. Cables to connect this to your TV should have gold-plated connectors (optional for enhanced quality). Following are step-by-step instructions on how to create this video.

1. Use double-faced tape to place photographs in chronological order on a black background against a wall. Using a video camera, videotape the photos at 4–5 seconds on each picture. Adjust with the "zoom" as needed, fade to black for endings, or blur. (*Alternative:* Instead of using photographs, you can use bits from other videos. Watch the video and take notes of the key spots you want to record. As the video tape you are taping from plays on VCR #1, hit *record* and *pause* on your editor.)

Using either one of these methods gives you Tape A in VCR #2.

2. Run Tape A (your new tape) in VCR #1 and using the stereo/audio mixer you have four tracks to —
    a. add music by playing a favorite song, record, or tape or having someone play live music.
    b. add your own narration to the picture.
    c. leave the original sound from the original tape.
    d. adjust the overall sound on the resulting tape.

3. If you want to get really deluxe, you can buy a character generator and put words on the screen, or you can use handlettered or computer-generated titles.

This setup makes a delightful photo album for someone very special to you. If you plan to sell your video, use live original music so as not to get in trouble with copyright infringement. If your results are applauded by those who view your tape, this could become a business idea for you. (See Appendix D: Starting a Business.)

Tour — Go on tours. Tour a beer brewery, a tea company, a glass factory, a model railroad layout, and so on.

Toys — Many organizations are providing stuffed toys to children involved in a police situation, traffic accident, domestic dispute, or other emergency. They sometimes call them "Toys of Love" and know that these gifts ease the children's pain. Start a program like this where you live.

Trade — Trade work with other people. "You paint my house, and I'll lay your tile," or any other trade you both like the sound of. Take a look at the world of trade underway at www.ebay.com.

Trains—Enjoy a trip on a train with your favorite travel buddy. Call Amtrak at 1-800-872-7245, or visit www.amtrak.com. Join a model railroaders group. Build layouts from kits. Visit train museums. Check out www.greatesthobby.com (1-877-426-5082).

Travel—Appendix F, Travel Tips, is full of travel tidbits, ideas, and information. To improve your equilibrium and balance while riding in a car, bus, or plane, refer to *Brain Gym®* Activities, Appendix C.

Travel Agent—Become a travel agent or tour guide. Check the Yellow Pages of a large city under *Travel or Tourism Development and Education*.

Trekkie—If you're a Star Trek fan, go to conventions displaying memorabilia. Meet and correspond with other "Trekkies." Visit www.treknation.com and click into TrekToday (daily updated guide to all things Star Trek) and Trek BBS (the largest community for Star Trek fans on the Internet, with over 5,000 members posting topics in a variety of forums).

Typing—Are you a retired secretary or word processor? Do you really love to type? Would you like to work out of your home? College students are always looking for someone to type their papers; job hunters need résumés created or updated; small offices sometimes have overflow work for freelancers. If you are a good typist, you can take in as much work as you like. It would be very helpful to have a computer and a letter quality printer. To improve your keyboard ability, refer to *Brain Gym®* Activities, Appendix C.

Unclutter—Clear out your life of things you don't need or use. Then have a garage sale and use the money you collect to do or buy something special for yourself. Alternatively, donate your goods or proceeds to a worthy cause. Visit www.mindoverclutter.com, www.beclutter-free.com, and www.allthatwomenwant.com/cluttercontrol.htm.

Vacation Spot—Stay at the charming Seth Peterson Cottage at Lake Delton, Wisconsin. It was designed by Frank Lloyd Wright and is one of his smallest and final creations. Contact the Sand County Service Co., at P.O. Box 409, Lake Delton, WI 53940 or call 1-800-822-7768. See pictures at the website of the conservancy that operates the cottage: www.sethpeterson.org.

Vampires—Rent the movie *Interview with the Vampire* or read an Anne Rice book. Study vampire bats and learn how they differ from other bats. Learn about the Vampire Empire (formerly the Count Dracula Fan Club) at www.benecke.com/vampire.html.

Vatican—Visit the Vatican and other holy places all around the world.

Vegas — Enjoy a few days in Las Vegas. Log onto the official Vegas travel site for information about hotels, shows, and area tours at www.vegas.com.

Veterans' Death and Burial Benefits — For veterans and their spouses, Uncle Sam provides free burial, marker, and flag in veterans' or state cemeteries. Call the Veterans Administration at 1-800-827-1000.

Video — Make your own "how-to" video of your specialty. Find a television station that plays this kind of video. Or make video tapes of parents, grandparents, and older relatives. Have them talk, move around, and tell a little about themselves. When these older people have died, the grandchildren and generations to come will enjoy knowing their ancestors, hearing their stories, and seeing their facial features and expressions. Several of the little ones in Tricia's family have asked, "What was Grandpa or Grandma like?" A video would really help. Prepare a script for discussion while you're taping. "What was life like when you were young? How did you and so-and-so meet? What was good, bad, sad about your life? What funny things happened? Tell about food, work, and historical events going on during your life." Once you've gone to the trouble of preparing this script, you can go right into business doing videos for other families and friends.

I *think high self-esteem is overrated. A little low self-esteem is actually quite good . . . maybe you're not the best, so you should work a little harder.*

—Jay Leno

Visit — Go see the scenic and historic spots in your state. Appreciate the natural beauty, the museums, the historic towns, the antique shops, and so on. Take pictures of where you have been and put these together in a photo album. One benefit of being retired is that you can go to these places during the week while everyone else is working, unless you prefer to be with crowds when you sightsee. The choice is yours! Most visitor spots offer discounted admission for seniors. Some are open free one day a week. Call ahead to ask.

Volunteer — Hospitals, charitable organizations, schools, civic groups, places of worship, animal welfare societies, and social service organizations are all in need of people to volunteer their time and talents. Volunteering doesn't have to be all-consuming, since you can work as much or little as you like. Whatever you do, the rewards will be many. The Peace Corps loves retirees and has many volunteers older than sixty-five. For other ideas, refer to Appendix E, Volunteering. In your local Yellow Pages, look under *Social Service Organizations*.

Wallpaper — Put up wallpaper or a border in a room that is special to you. Try stenciling for an inexpensive alternative to wallpaper.

Weather Lore — This is an interesting area to study. Find out what significance folks see in the early migration of birds, an abundance of hummingbirds, the locusts' six-weeks-until-winter warning, the early ripening of chokecherries and raspberries, the rings on a woolly caterpillar, and so on. Talk to folks about weather lore, or read up on it at the library. Write an article or talk to a group about the weather lore you discover.

Weddings — Become a wedding consultant. Help make that "special day" come together for your clients. If you absolutely love to plan weddings, this could be a very rewarding career. The more you know about etiquette, religious protocols, and local retailers and services, the easier your job will be.

Marriage: It's like a cultural hand-rail. It links folks to the past and guides them to the future.

—Diane Frolov and Andrew Schneider

"Weekend" Sections of Newspapers — These sections publicize all kinds of things to do. They may list comedy-drama theater, musicals, dinner theaters, and a plethora of events from antique shows to tours of different restaurants. There are listings for dancing, including ballroom, senior, single, old-time, no-partner-needed, folk, round, country, hula, disco, Irish, Israeli folk, moving meditation, barn, polka, and swing. Some events are nonalcoholic and nonsmoking. Different weekend sections also list auditions; nightclubs categorized by jazz, rock, country, crossover, and comedy; art shows and art galleries; nature sites and events; kids' stuff; and museum events.

Where Can I Find? Columns — Read the "Wanted" sections of local publications to see what people want to buy. You might want to begin producing or collecting and selling items in high demand.

White Water Rafting — Is it in your future?

Widows/Widowers — Join a group for widows or widowers, called WOWs, or join Parents Without Partners. Join a singles club or go to singles dances.

Helping Them Cope: When a husband or wife dies is a very trying time. Friends usually send a sympathy card or flowers, attend the funeral or memorial service, and take food for the luncheon. Afterward, there are many things you can do. Offer to help the widow/widower send out the acknowledgment cards. The person is usually very grateful for that assistance, since it makes a grim job bearable. Tricia and her husband, Bill, offer to sort through and dispose of the deceased person's belongings. Give the widow/widower some time—it may take weeks or months—but when they're ready, go through everything from jewelry to junk, tools to treasures. Have a garage sale. Help dispose of collectibles, if that is your field of expertise. Otherwise, find a knowledgeable, trustworthy person to do it. Dispose of unwanted vehicles. Help the widow/widower buy a new(er) car to begin their new life. In the ensuing months, call them often. Encourage them to find new activities—golf, bridge, dancing, hobbies, travel—or possibly to move to a more suitable residence. Introduce them to others whose company they may enjoy. In time you may be welcoming their new boy/girlfriend. A friend of ours was seventy when his wife died. He said, "I figure I've only got ten more years, so I'm not going to waste a minute of it."

Wildlife—Work with wildlife in some way. Contact the Fish & Wildlife Service, the Interior Department, or the National Park Service, all listed in the phone book under United States Government.

Wills and Living Wills—These are important. Do you have them? A majority of Americans do *not.* The laws vary from state to state with regard to wills and living wills. If you have a living will, carry a copy with you. A living will won't do you any good sitting in your safe deposit box while you're lying in another state. See the entry "Legal Services Made Affordable" earlier in this book.

Women Golfers — Subscribe to *Golf for Women* by calling 1-800-962-5513 or going to www.golfdigest.com/gfw. Every issue offers interesting and helpful articles about your game and places to play. You'll also find ads for custom-tailored clubs, instruction, and just about anything else a woman golfer could want. Also visit www.ladygolf.com (1-888-215-5855) or www.sporthaley.com (1-800-627-9211).

It took me seventeen years to get three thousand hits in baseball. I did it in one afternoon on the golf course.

—Hank Aaron

Women Keep Active — Studies show that women who exercise after menopause live longer than sedentarywomen. Bowling, gardening, walking four or more times a week, and weightbearing and weightlifting exercises for stronger bones, increase a woman's lifespan by a substantial percentage. Moderate activity (once a week) also increases a woman's lifespan, but by a smaller percentage.

Woodworking — Maybe you dream of building the projects you see in *Popular Woodworking* magazine (www.popularwoodworking.com), in your local newspaper, or on the PBS stations. Go for it.

Work — Do you want to work with babies, children, teens, adults, or old people? Do you work better with sick people or well people? Good kids or troubled kids? At-risk kids? Criminals or gangs? Find ways to help others by offering your services as a baby-sitter, an advocate, a hotline operator, or a caregiver. Look for ads and fliers requesting help; these often appear on public bulletin boards, at bus stops, and in newspapers. Local television stations may air agency requests for volunteers. Some organizations and individuals will pay for your time and services.

The greatest conflicts are not between two people but between one person and himself.

—Garth Brooks

Wrinkle-Free Botox— Do away with your wrinkles, if you want to. See a dermatologist or plastic surgeon for injections of Botox (actually, the same toxin that causes botulism). A full-forehead Botox treatment can make you look younger, calmer, happier, and friendlier. The Botox treatment is only good for four months and needs to be repeated. Plastic surgery is more permanent. Ask your doctor about risks and side effects. Also investigate other types of face-lift or cosmetic surgery. Also visit www.hydroderm.com.

Write—

Autobiography: Write an autobiography or put together a family history. Each of us has our own "story," if we would just take the time to put it in writing. Children and grandchildren particularly enjoy hearing about their ancestors' early years. Once Grandma and Grandpa were young and in love, too, and just starting their lives together. Once they were children who played and argued. Future generations can enjoy and learn

Not only is your story worth telling, but it can be told in words so painstakingly eloquent that it becomes a song.

—Gloria Naylor

from your memories and experiences, if you record them. Adult and continuing education programs offer courses that can help you write and publish your personal and family histories.

Book: Do something crazy, scary, wild, and wonderful, and then write a book about it. Mike McIntyre hitchhiked from Cape Fear, North Carolina, to the Golden Gate Bridge. He went without money and accepted only rides, food, and a place to rest his head. His story became *The Kindness of Strangers* (Berkley). Read *The Best American Travel Writing 2005* by Kincaid and Wilson (Houghton Mifflin) and *Bold Spirit: Helga Estby's Forgotten Walk Across Victorian America* by Linda Lawrence Hunt (Anchor).

Commercials, Slogans, Jingles: Put your creative hat on and make some up. Then send them to the appropriate businesses.

Essays: Write essays about anything and everything, the way Charles Osgood of "The Osgood Files" does (www.theosgoodfiles.com). Sell them to a radio syndicate for broadcast on the radio or to a newspaper syndicate for publication.

Mystery Stories for Kids: Could you be the next J. K. Rowling, the best-selling author of the Harry Potter series? What an unbelievable notoriety she has enjoyed because of her intensely imaginative storylines. And we all remember R. L. Stine and the Goosebumps and Fear Street series, written for kids ages eight to twelve. Thanks to both of these authors, millions of children have taken a shine to reading. It is hoped that this passion for reading will continue on to more "literary" works as these young readers mature. Another children's series is Hoot, one of many mysteries written by Carl Hiaasen (Knopf Books for Young Readers). Is there a story waiting inside you? (www.childrensbooks.about.com)

Play: Are you tired of seeing *Auntie Mame, Oklahoma,* and *Nunsense* for the umpteenth time? To improve your creative writing ability, refer to *Brain Gym*® Activities, Appendix C.

Xerox—Make xerographic copies of letters and exchange them with members of your family and friends in round-robin fashion.

Yarn—Consider making blankets and all kinds of knitted goods for people in need of warmth and comfort. For information on how to knit and free patterns, visit www.knitting.about.com.

Yellowstone—Visit Yellowstone National Park in either summer or winter and attend interesting field courses that are taught by experts. For more information, contact the Yellowstone Association Institute at P.O. Box 117, Yellowstone National Park, WY 82190. You can also call them at 1-307-344-2293 or see what is available on their website at www.yellowstoneassociation.org. To order books, maps, videos, and other educational products, call 1-877-967-0090.

Yoga—Learn yoga and meditation for relaxation. Go online and explore www.yogasite.com, "an eclectic collection of yogic connections."

You've Tried a Dozen Things — Keep trying, even if you've tried a dozen ways to make extra money and not one has panned out. Perhaps you've been poo-pooed for everything you've tried or even talked about. Don't give up. As a friend of ours always said, "If you throw enough things against the wall, one's bound to stick sooner or later." Keep trying.

Yo-yo — Teach youngsters how to do tricks with a yo-yo. Keep up-to-date with what's new in yoyoing at www.yoyo.com.

Zip — Zip through the house periodically, cleaning and tidying up.

Zippedy — Sing "Zippedy-Do-Dah," "Mairzy Doats," "Supercalifragilisticexpialidosious," "Abba Dabba Honeymoon," and other silly songs. Better yet, teach them to your grandchildren. Best of all, dance while you're singing.

There's no point in being grown up if you can't be childish sometimes.

—Doctor Who

Zoo — Zoos are great places for the young and old. Many zoos have free days for seniors weekly or several times a year. See if your local zoo needs help with tours, especially during the school year when field trips to the zoo are popular.

Zucchini Bread—What do you do with all that zucchini in your garden? Grate some and freeze it, putting two cups of grated zucchini into each freezer bag. Then pull out a bag of the pre-measured zucchini any time during the year, and make yourself two loaves of zucchini bread! The recipe follows:

> Beat together well:
>> 3 eggs
>> 2 cups sugar
>> 1 cup oil
>
> Add:
>> 1 teaspoon vanilla
>> 3 cups flour
>> 1 teaspoon each of cinnamon,
>>> salt, and baking powder
>> 1/4 teaspoon baking soda
>> 2 cups grated zucchini
>> 1 cup crushed nuts or crushed drained pineapple

Pour batter into two greased and floured bread pans and bake at 350 degrees for one hour, or until knife comes out clean. If you make the bread with the pineapple, add an extra touch of flour. Barb sometimes adds grated coconut and granola cereal in place of the nuts and pineapple.

LET YOUR IMAGINATION SOAR

ACTIVITIES FROM

 A TO Z

Partake of a smorgasbord of exciting ideas and activities! The following list gives cryptic explanations designed to pique your interest and whet your appetite for further study or action. Subjects run the gamut from *abacus* to *zymurgy*. Look for ideas that interest you, even remotely, and mark them for consideration now or sometime in the future. (If this is a library book, splurge and get your own copy to mark, or use a notebook.)

Topic	Interested?			Remarks
	Yes	No	Later	
ABACUS Learn to use one.				
ABALONE Buy jewelry made of abalone shell; fish for/eat abalone.				
ABROAD Travel to foreign countries.				
ABSTRACT Study/create abstract art.				
ABUSE Help abused men/women/children.				
ACCORDION Learn to play the accordion.				
ACROBATICS Teach/coach acrobatics.				
ACTIVE Stay active/alert/sociable.				

Topic	Interested?			Remarks
	Yes	No	Later	
ACUPUNCTURE Study/try as treatment for pain.				
ADDICT Work with drug addicts.				
AEROBICS Exercise your lungs and heart.				
AFGHAN Knit/crochet an afghan for your naps.				
AFRICA Study African history/culture/issues.				
AIRPLANE Collect/build/fly model airplanes.				
ALCOHOLISM Don't drink much; help someone who drinks too much.				
ALLIGATOR Go alligator hunting.				
AMARYLLIS Give someone this lovely plant.				
AMERICA Study/teach American history or geography.				

Topic	Interested?			Remarks
	Yes	No	Later	
AMPUTEE Help someone less fortunate.				
AMUSE Learn to amuse yourself and/or others.				
ANIMAL Offer to walk people's dogs; baby-sit people's hamsters/birds/fish.				
ANTARCTIC Study the region south of the Antarctic Circle.				
ANTARES Study the giant red star in the constellation Scorpio.				
APHID Learn about gardening/insects/diseases.				
ARTIST Learn to create pictures/sculptures.				
AUCTION Buy/sell items at auction, or just attend one.				
AUDIENCE Be a part of the audience of your favorite talk show.				

Topic	Interested?			Remarks
	Yes	No	Later	
AUSTRALIA Visit Australia; study penal colony history.				
AVATAR Study Hindu mythology.				
BABEL Study this Biblical city.				
BABY-SIT Sit grandchildren/neighbors' children occasionally.				
BAGUETTE Study/buy/sell gems; make jewelry.				
BAIZE Restore pool table; cover with this fabric.				
BAKE Learn to cook/bake.				
BALKAN PENINSULA Study/visit Greece or Turkey.				
BAND Form a group of musicians; entertain.				
BANJO Learn to play the banjo.				

Topic	Interested?			Remarks
	Yes	No	Later	
BARBECUE Have a barbecue; invite friends.				
BARBELL Exercise/weight train.				
BARBERSHOP Join a quartet; entertain others.				
BARTENDER Work as a bartender.				
BASEBALL Play/coach/attend baseball games.				
BASILICA Study/visit famous cathedrals/ basilicas.				
BATTERY Replace the battery in your car.				
BEACHCOMBER Walk/vacation on the beach.				
BEDRIDDEN Visit/read to/cheer up bedridden people.				
BESTSELLER Read; join a book club; discuss books.				
BICYCLE Ride for fun and exercise.				

Topic	Interested?			Remarks
	Yes	No	Later	
BLINTZ Make thin pancakes folded over cheese or fruit.				
BLOOD BANK Volunteer/give blood.				
BODY LANGUAGE Perceive attitudes that are communicated through body language.				
BOOMERANG Buy curved missile that returns to thrower.				
BORSCHT Make beet soup hot or cold.				
BOW Practice shooting arrows.				
BOXER Study Chinese secret society action of 1900.				
BOXING Watch/teach/coach boxing.				
BRAILLE Study/teach braille.				
BRAINSTORM Share ideas/inspiration with others.				

HOW TO ENJOY YOUR RETIREMENT

Topic	Interested?			Remarks
	Yes	No	Later	
BRASS BAND Listen to/join a brass band.				
BRONTOSAURUS Study dinosaurs of the Jurassic period.				
BUDDHISM Study the doctrines of this Eastern religion.				
BULL MARKET Follow the stock market.				
BYZANTIUM Learn about the ancient city on the site of Istanbul.				
CABINETMAKER Make/buy fine wood furniture.				
CACTUS Visit a desert in springtime.				
CALLIGRAPHY Study/practice beautiful penmanship.				
CAMARADERIE Enjoy friendly good will among comrades.				
CAMPAIGN Work for/against political candidates.				

Topic	Interested?			Remarks
	Yes	No	Later	
CARTOON Learn how to draw cartoons.				
CASINO Have fun gambling (if you can control it!).				
CATALOG Order merchandise from a catalog.				
CAUCUS Attend a political caucus.				
CENTERPIECE Create a gorgeous centerpiece for your table.				
CERAMICS Learn to make ceramics/pottery/porcelain.				
CHEMOTHERAPY Help/visit someone taking chemotherapy.				
CHESS Play chess; enter tournaments.				
CHILI CON CARNE Enter a chili-making or chili-eating contest.				
CHIPPENDALE Study/buy rococo/18th-century furniture.				

Topic	Interested?			Remarks
	Yes	No	Later	
CHRISTIANITY Study the history of Christianity.				
CIRCUS Attend a circus/pageant/fair.				
CIVIL WAR Study the Civil War.				
CLAY PIGEON Try trapshooting.				
CLEF Learn to read/play music.				
CLIMATOLOGY Study the science of climates.				
CLUTCH Fix/repair your car.				
COAT OF ARMS Study your family coat of arms/heraldry.				
COLOSSEUM Visit the Roman amphitheater.				
COMIC BOOK Collect/buy/sell/trade comic books.				
COMMON MARKET Study the European Economic Community.				

Topic	Interested?			Remarks
	Yes	No	Later	
COMPLEMENT Find a friend and provide for each other's needs.				
CONGRESS Write/call your senator/ representative.				
CONSOLE Comfort someone in sorrow.				
CONTESTANT Be a contestant on your favorite TV game show.				
CONTINENTAL CONGRESS Study legislative bodies of 1774–1781.				
COPPERHEAD Study North American snakes.				
COPYRIGHT Write something and obtain a copyright.				
COUNTRY DANCE Learn to country/line/square dance.				
COUSIN Get together with your cousin(s).				
COVERED WAGON Study the American pioneers.				

Topic	Interested?			Remarks
	Yes	No	Later	
CPR Take a course to get/renew your cardiopulmonary resuscitation certificate.				
CRANIOLOGY Study the structure/characteristics of skulls.				
CREATIVE Create something new/new ways to do things.				
CREWEL Learn this form of embroidery.				
CRICKET Play cricket with bat, ball, and wickets.				
CRIMINOLOGY Study crime/criminals; visit prisoners.				
CRO-MAGNON Study prehistoric human found in France.				
CROQUET Play croquet with wooden mallets and balls.				
CROSS-COUNTRY SKI Go cross-country skiing.				

Topic	Interested?			Remarks
	Yes	No	Later	
CRUISE Take a nice cruise.				
CUBA Study Cuba's history/politics/problems.				
CURLING IRON Use a curling iron on your hair.				
DAGUERREOTYPE Study early photographic process.				
DAR Join Daughters of the American Revolution.				
DARTS Throw darts at a bull's-eye; join a dart league.				
DEBRIS Remove debris from a garden/vacant lot/river.				
DECLARATION OF INDEPENDENCE Read it again.				
DELFT Collect blue-and-white tableware.				

Topic	Interested?			Remarks
	Yes	No	Later	
DENDROLOGY Study trees.				
DESIGN Design your new house/ clothing/decor.				
DIABETES Be checked for diabetes.				
DIAMOND Sell/collect diamonds/jewelry.				
DILL PICKLE Make a crock of dill pickles.				
DIORAMA Build a miniature scene with figures and background.				
DIRIGIBLE Study lighter-than-air aircraft.				
DO IT YOURSELF Build something in the house.				
DOLL Collect/buy/sell/refurbish dolls.				
DRAWERS Clean drawers in bedroom/ kitchen/file cabinet.				
DRIVE Take the 55-Alive or similar defensive driving course.				

Topic	Interested?			Remarks
	Yes	No	Later	
DROMEDARY Ride/photograph a camel.				
DUDE Visit a dude ranch.				
ECLECTIC Decorate with several styles of furniture.				
ECLIPSE Watch/study/travel to see the next eclipse.				
EGYPTOLOGY Study antiquities of Egypt.				
ELECTRICITY Study electricity.				
ELIZABETHAN Study Elizabeth I of England.				
EMBROIDER Learn to embroider.				
EMMY Watch Emmy awards on TV.				
ENGLISH Help someone speak/read.				
ENVIRONMENTALIST Work to improve the environment.				

Topic	Interested?			Remarks
	Yes	No	Later	
EPISCOPAL Study/attend the Episcopal Church.				
EQUATION Help/tutor students in math.				
ESP Improve your extrasensory perception.				
EULOGY Give a eulogy at a funeral.				
EVANGELIST Study the New Testament.				
EXHIBIT Display your collection of ???.				
EYE Have your eyes checked regularly.				
FACE-LIFT Have a face-lift/tummy tuck/ whatever you want.				
FAIR Attend/enter a state/county fair.				
FAIRY TALE Read one to a child; write a new one.				

Topic	Interested?			Remarks
	Yes	No	Later	
FAUST Read a version of the German legend.				
FEUDALISM Study the medieval European system.				
FIRE ALARM Replace the batteries in your fire alarms.				
FIREPLACE Change your fireplace to gas/ electric.				
FIX Do repairs around your house.				
FLAGSTONE Build a patio/walkway/ fountain/barbecue.				
FLUTE Learn to play the flute.				
FOLKLORE Study folk cultures of differ- ent countries.				
FOOTBALL Watch/coach football.				
FORTY-NINER Study pioneers in 1849 gold rush.				

Topic	Interested?			Remarks
	Yes	No	Later	
FOURTEENERS Climb mountains over 14,000 feet.				
FREEMASON Join a Masonic lodge.				
FRIENDSHIP To have a friend, be a friend.				
FÜHRER Study Adolf Hitler.				
FURNITURE Redecorate; rearrange your furniture.				
GAME BIRD Hunt pheasant/duck/partridge/geese.				
GANG Work with at-risk youth/gang members.				
GENEALOGY Trace your family tree.				
GENTLEMAN FARMER Own the farm and let others work it.				
GEOLOGICAL TIME SCALE Study eras/epochs of earth history.				

Topic	Interested?			Remarks
	Yes	No	Later	
GERMAN Learn the language; travel to Germany.				
GOLF Play/enter tournaments.				
GOTHIC Study Gothic architecture; read a Gothic novel.				
GOURMET Become a gourmet cook; watch one on TV.				
GRAFFITI Report to police; paint over graffiti.				
GREAT LAKES Visit all five Great Lakes.				
GREGORIAN CHANT Listen to Gregorian chant.				
GROSS NATIONAL PRODUCT Study national economics.				
GUILLOTINE Study the French Revolution.				
GUITAR Learn to play guitar; join a band.				

Topic	Interested?			Remarks
	Yes	No	Later	
GUN CONTROL Decide where you stand on this issue.				
GUTTER Clean out/replace/paint your gutters.				
HAIRDRESSER Be your own hairdresser; do others' hair.				
HAITI Study Haiti's history/culture/problems.				
HALFWAY HOUSE Inquire about rules governing a nearby halfway house.				
HALIBUT Eat more fish; take fish oil pills.				
HANDBALL Play handball at the gym with friends.				
HANDICAP Try to lower your bowling/golf handicap.				
HANDICAPPED Work with/help handicapped people.				

Topic	Interested?			Remarks
	Yes	No	Later	
HAWAII Enjoy a trip to Hawaii; compare the different islands.				
HEART Protect your heart: eat right/ exercise/relax.				
HELICOPTER Take a helicopter flight; learn to fly.				
HERBS Study/grow/use herbs.				
HESSIAN Study the American Revolution.				
HIEROGLYPHIC Study Egyptian history/ culture/writing.				
HOCKEY Teach/coach/watch hockey.				
HOMELESS Work with/feed the homeless.				
HOMEOPATHY Try homeopathy to cure your ills.				
HONEYBEE Raise honeybees; sell honey.				

Topic	Interested?			Remarks
	Yes	No	Later	
HONKY-TONK Learn to play honky-tonk/ ragtime piano.				
HORSE Buy/sell/own/ride horses; attend races (but see entry PARI-MUTUEL).				
HOTTENTOT Study African history/Bush- men and Bantu cultures.				
HOVERCRAFT Ride in one over land and water.				
HULA Learn to do this Hawaiian dance.				
HUMMINGBIRD Put out/watch the action at a hummingbird feeder.				
HUNGARY Study Hungary's history/ culture/language.				
HURRICANE Help victims of a hurricane.				
HYACINTH Plant bulbs; enjoy results in the spring.				

Topic	Interested?			Remarks
	Yes	No	Later	
HYDROPONICS Grow plants without soil.				
HYPERTENSION Have your blood pressure checked.				
HYPOTENUSE Learn/teach geometry.				
ICE SKATE Attend an ice show; skate on a pond or in a rink.				
ILLITERACY Teach people to read.				
IMMIGRANT Work with immigrants; take a stand on illegal immigration.				
IMPRESSIONISM Study 19th-century art/ literature/music.				
INCANDESCENT LAMP Change to energy-saving fluorescents.				
INCEST Help victims of incest.				
INCORPORATE Incorporate your business.				

Topic	Interested?			Remarks
	Yes	No	Later	
INDIA Learn about/visit India; buy Indian goods.				
INFORMATION Work in an information booth at an airport or a fair.				
INTERIOR DECORATOR Take a class in interior design; hire a decorator.				
INVESTMENTS Keep yours appropriate for retirement.				
INVITATION Invite friends over often, whether or not they reciprocate.				
IONIC Study Greek architecture/ scrolls/columns.				
IRON AGE Study the Iron/Bronze/Stone Age(s).				
ISLAM Study the religion of the Muslims.				
ISSUE Form educated opinions about issues of the day.				

Topic	Interested?			Remarks
	Yes	No	Later	
JACK-OF-ALL-TRADES Become a handyperson.				
JACKPOT Buy (low-cost) lottery tickets; win jackpots.				
JACKS Play jacks with children.				
JAM SESSION Have fun playing an instru- ment with other musicians.				
JAPAN Study Japanese history/ culture.				
JEWELRY Buy/make/sell/collect one form or various forms of jewelry.				
JIGSAW PUZZLE Work puzzles.				
JINNI Study Muslim mythology.				
JITTERBUG Dance a good, fast jitterbug.				
JOURNAL Keep a journal/diary.				

Topic	Interested?			Remarks
	Yes	No	Later	
JUGGLE Learn to juggle; entertain others.				
JUJITSU Learn Japanese unarmed self-defense.				
JUROR Serve on a jury.				
JUVENILE Work with juveniles.				
KACHINA Study ancestral spirits/dolls of Native Americans.				
KARATE Learn self-defense.				
KAYAK Learn/teach how to use a kayak.				
KAZOO Play in a kazoo band.				
KENNEL Build/volunteer at a kennel.				
KERMESS Attend a carnival/festival in Belgium or the Netherlands.				

Topic	Interested?			Remarks
	Yes	No	Later	
KETTLEDRUM Learn/teach how to play a kettledrum.				
KIBBUTZ Study collective farming in Israel.				
KILT What do they wear under them?				
KINETIC ENERGY Learn about/teach energy in motion, from electric currents to waterfalls.				
KNIGHTS OF COLUMBUS Join the fraternal society of Roman Catholic men.				
KNIGHTS TEMPLAR Learn about the society of Free and Accepted Masons.				
KNOT Learn/teach how to tie square knots/bowknots.				
LABOR Do some healthy, safe physical labor; be a Lamaze or labor coach for expectant mothers.				

Topic	Interested?			Remarks
	Yes	No	Later	
LABORATORY Do scientific research.				
LACE Make lace; teach others how to make lace.				
LAITY Help out at your place of worship.				
LAMINATE Make layers of wood/plastic for woodcrafts, plaques, menus, maps, and ID cards.				
LANCELOT Act in a play/show.				
LAND FILL Complain about hazardous waste-dumping.				
LANDSCAPE Paint/photograph/landscape your yard.				
LANGUAGE Learn/teach a new language.				
LAP DOG Get a very small dog.				
LAUGH And the world laughs with you!				

Topic	Interested?			Remarks
	Yes	No	Later	
LAUNCHING PAD Build model rockets.				
LAYER CAKE Learn/teach how to bake/ decorate cakes.				
LEADERSHIP Train in/teach leadership skills.				
LEARN Learn a new skill/craft/ occupation/hobby.				
LECTURE Speak publicly about your favorite subject.				
LEGISLATION Monitor the state legislature.				
LEPRECHAUN Study Irish folklore.				
LETTERS Write praise/complaint letters to companies.				
LIP READ Learn/teach lip reading.				
LIVEN UP Liven up your own or someone else's life.				

Topic	Interested?			Remarks
	Yes	No	Later	
LOAF Spend some time lazily.				
LOBSTER Cook lobster; invite friends.				
LUFTWAFFE Learn about the German Air Force in WWII.				
LUGGAGE Pack up and go somewhere you want to see.				
LURE Make your own fishing lures; try them out.				
MACBETH Read Shakespeare.				
MAGIC Perform magic tricks.				
MAH-JONGG Learn to play this Chinese game.				
MALAPROPISM Misuse words; send examples to *Reader's Digest*.				
MAMBO Learn this rumba-like dance.				

Topic	Interested?			Remarks
	Yes	No	Later	
MANUSCRIPT Write that steamy novel.				
MARKSMAN Practice sport shooting.				
MARXISM/LENINISM Study history/politics of Germany/Russia.				
MASTERMIND Plan/execute a project skillfully.				
MASTER OF CEREMONY Preside over entertainment or dinner.				
MAYA Visit a Mayan temple.				
MAYFLOWER Learn about the pilgrims.				
MAYOR Run for mayor.				
MECHANIC Fix things for yourself/others.				
MEMORY Improve your memory/ concentration.				
MENTAL RETARDATION Work with people with mental retardation.				

Topic	Interested?			Remarks
	Yes	No	Later	
MENTOR Be a mentor/guide to someone.				
MILE Walk a mile or two every day.				
MILKY WAY Learn/teach about the solar system.				
MIME Narrate without words (pantomime).				
MINCE PIE Enter your favorite recipe in a contest/fair.				
MONOCHROME Paint or draw in a single color.				
MORSE CODE Learn/teach Morse code.				
MUSICIAN Learn to play a/another musical instrument.				
MUZZLE LOADER Collect antique firearms.				
NAACP Work for organizations devoted to advancing the rights of people of color.				

Topic	Interested?			Remarks
	Yes	No	Later	
NAP It's okay to take a nap after retirement (and even before!).				
NARRATE Tell stories to someone.				
NATIVE AMERICAN Study the history and culture of a tribe.				
NATURAL HISTORY Study animals/plants/minerals.				
NATURAL RESOURCE Work to protect soil/forests/ endangered species/water.				
NATURE Study the physical universe and its phenomena.				
NAUTICAL Study ships/sailors/navigation.				
NEGOTIATE Bargain for what you want.				
NEIGHBOR Meet and make friends with neighbors.				
NESTOR Read what this wise old king did in the Trojan War.				

Topic	Interested?			Remarks
	Yes	No	Later	
NETWORK Build a support network of friends/associates/helpers; use/ join a computer network such as America Online or Prodigy.				
NEUROLOGY Study the nervous system.				
NEW DEAL Study President F. D. Roosevelt's policies.				
NEW/OLD TESTAMENT Take a Bible study class.				
NEW ZEALAND Study/visit New Zealand.				
NICKEL Start a coin collection.				
NICKELODEON Buy/repair/collect jukeboxes.				
NIRVANA Learn about the ideals and goal of Buddhism.				
NOCTURNAL Study animals/flowers that come out at night.				
NOISE Learn about noise stress and reduce yours.				

Topic	Interested?			Remarks
	Yes	No	Later	
NONVOTER Convince a nonvoter to vote.				
NORSE Study Scandinavian culture.				
NORTHUMBRIA Study ancient Anglo-Saxon Britain.				
NORTH VIETNAM Study the causes/effects of the Vietnam War.				
NOTE Learn to read music.				
NOUGAT Make this candy with honey and pistachios.				
NOVELTY Manufacture/sell trinkets.				
NUCLEAR ENERGY Learn about this energy alternative; stand for or against.				
NUDISM Investigate this philosophy— is it for you?				
NURSE Become a nurse; help someone who is ill.				

Topic	Interested?			Remarks
	Yes	No	Later	
NURSING HOME Visit/entertain the elderly.				
NUTRITION Study nutrition; eat properly.				
OBEDIENCE Take your dog to obedience school.				
OBERON Study medieval folklore.				
OBITUARY Write/call people before you find their names in the obituary.				
OBSERVE Take time to see/enjoy your world.				
OCELOT Visit a zoo or natural history museum.				
OCTET Play in a group of eight musical performers.				
OCTOPUS Study marine life.				
ODIN Study Norse mythology.				

Topic	Interested?			Remarks
	Yes	No	Later	
ODYSSEY Read/enjoy Homer's epic poem.				
OIL Follow/buy some oil stock.				
OIL PAINT Try this easy form of painting.				
OLD WORLD Visit Europe or Asia				
OLYMPIC GAMES Attend/watch/work for the Olympic Games.				
OMELET Make eggs folded over something tasty.				
OPAL Study/sell/collect gems.				
OP ART Study 1960s art and geometric/ optical illusions.				
OPEN-HEARTED Be candid and kind.				
OPERA Enjoy an opera/operetta.				
OPPORTUNITY Be open/ready when oppor- tunity knocks.				

Topic	Interested?			Remarks
	Yes	No	Later	
OPTIMISM Keep a cheerful attitude.				
ORCHARD Grow fruit/nut/olive trees.				
ORCHESTRA Play in/listen to an orchestra.				
ORCHID Raise orchids; enter contests; join a society.				
ORIENT Visit/study/invest in Asia/the East.				
ORION Study constellations and mythology.				
OROGENY Study the process of mountain formation.				
ORPHEUS Read about him in Greek mythology.				
ORWELLIAN Read the writings of satirist George Orwell.				
OSPREY Observe/study this large hawk that feeds on fish.				

Topic	Interested?			Remarks
	Yes	No	Later	
OSTEOLOGY Study the functions of bones.				
OTTER Observe/learn about this swimming mammal with webbed feet.				
OUIJA Play on the board/spell out telepathic messages.				
OUTBOARD Buy/ride in a motorboat.				
OUTDOORS Enjoy the great outdoors.				
OXTAIL Buy one and make soup.				
OXYMORON Use/create combinations of contradictory words.				
OYSTER Enjoy fresh oysters/oyster stew.				
OZONE Learn about the upper atmosphere.				
PAGODA Visit the Far East; see a tower used as a temple.				

Topic	Interested?			Remarks
	Yes	No	Later	
PAINT Paint rooms/houses/pictures.				
PALESTINE Study the history/politics of Palestine.				
PALETTE KNIFE Mix and apply artist's colors.				
PALMISTRY Read the past/future in the palm of your hand.				
PAMPHLET Write/distribute political pamphlets.				
PANAMA CANAL Take a trip through the canal.				
PANEL DISCUSSION Moderate/participate in a panel discussion.				
PANELING Remove paneling; panel a wall.				
PANORAMA Enjoy/photograph/paint a lovely view.				
PANSY Grow pansies.				

Topic	Interested?			Remarks
	Yes	No	Later	
PAPACY Study the Roman Catholic government.				
PAPER HANGER Paper some walls; hang wallpaper borders.				
PAR Play golf with friends.				
PARACHUTE Did you have a golden one?				
PARADE Design/build/ride on parade floats.				
PARAGRAPH Your novel/letter begins with the paragraph.				
PARAKEET Buy a parakeet/parrot.				
PARAPSYCHOLOGY Study telepathy/ESP/psychic phenomena.				
PARI-MUTUEL Bet only what you can afford to lose.				
PARK Walk in/help build a park.				

Topic	Interested?			Remarks
	Yes	No	Later	
PARKINSON'S DISEASE Help someone with this disease.				
PARQUET Install some inlaid woodwork.				
PARTHENON See the Acropolis at Athens.				
PASTA Make/eat pasta; open an Italian restaurant.				
PASTEL Draw with colored pencils.				
PASTE-UP Publish a newsletter.				
PATROL Ride along with the police/ sheriff/fire department.				
PAUNCH Watch that waistline.				
PEARL Dive for pearls; make pearl jewelry.				
PEDDLE Sell small wares.				
PEDICURE Care for your own/someone else's feet.				

Topic	Interested?			Remarks
	Yes	No	Later	
PEDIGREE Buy/show/raise purebred dogs.				
PENITENTIARY Visit a prison.				
PENMANSHIP Teach penmanship; write letters for someone.				
PENTATHLON Enter an athletic contest of five events.				
PERIODIC TABLE Study chemistry.				
PERSUASION Practice the art of persuasion.				
PETROGRAPHY Describe and classify rocks.				
PEWTER Make/collect pewter figures.				
PHAETON Ride in/buy an early, open, two-seat automobile.				
PHARMACOLOGY Study the uses/effects of drugs.				
PHILATELY Collect postage stamps and stamped envelopes.				

Topic	Interested?			Remarks
	Yes	No	Later	
PHOBIA Study/try hypnotism as therapy for fears.				
PHONICS Teach spelling/reading using phonics.				
PHONOGRAPH Tape your old phonograph records.				
PHYSICAL EDUCATION Train/develop athletes.				
PHYSICAL THERAPY Make use of ice/heat/massage/exercise/rest.				
PHYSIOGNOMY Study how facial features reveal character.				
PIANO/KEYBOARD Learn to entertain yourself/others.				
PICTOGRAPH Draw a picture representing an idea.				
PIG Get a cute little piggy for a pet.				
PIGEON Raise/race pigeons.				

Topic	Interested?			Remarks
	Yes	No	Later	
PILGRIMAGE Go on a pilgrimage.				
PILOT Learn to fly a plane.				
PINEAPPLE Make a fancy dish with fresh pineapple.				
PINECONE Make a holiday decoration/ wreath.				
PINOCHLE Play this great card game.				
PIPE DREAM Daydreaming is okay.				
PITCHMAN Sell small articles at a fair.				
PIZZAZZ Live life with flair/irresistible charm.				
PLAID Study plaids of the Scottish Highlands.				
PLAN Make plans for your day, week, and year and for a special event.				

Topic	Interested?			Remarks
	Yes	No	Later	
PLANET Study the planets/universe.				
PLANTAGENET Study the British royal family from Henry II to the Tudor era.				
PLASTER OF PARIS Make molds/statuary/train layout.				
PLAYHOUSE Build a playhouse for kids.				
PLEASE Please yourself/your significant other.				
PLUMBING Repair your plumbing.				
POETRY Read/write/enjoy poetry.				
POINSETTIA Try to get one to turn red again.				
POKER Enjoy playing cards with friends.				
POLAND Learn the language/travel to Poland.				

Topic	Interested?			Remarks
	Yes	No	Later	
POLARIS Study the star that stays in fixed position.				
POLISH Polish your furniture/car.				
POLKA Learn/enjoy the polka.				
POLL Take a poll or census.				
POLO Try this game on horseback.				
POMOLOGY Study the science of fruit culture.				
POOL Swim for fun and relaxation; shoot pool with friends; pool funds and splurge.				
POP ART Study painting that looks like comic strips.				
PORK BARREL Monitor spending in the legislature.				
POSITIVE Maintain a positive attitude.				

Topic	Interested?			Remarks
	Yes	No	Later	
PRETZEL Enjoy a chewy, plump, warm one with a cold beer or soda pop.				
PULSE Take someone's pulse for them.				
PUPPET Put on a puppet show.				
PURL Learn to knit and purl.				
PURSUE Do something you always wanted to do.				
PUTTER Putter around the house and yard.				
PUZZLE Work puzzles to keep your mind alert.				
PYRAMID Study the Egyptian pyramids.				
QUADRILLE Learn/teach a square dance for four couples.				
QUAIL Hunt/eat quail.				

Topic	Interested?			Remarks
	Yes	No	Later	
QUAKER Learn about the Society of Friends.				
QUARREL Mend a quarrel if you can.				
QUARTET Play instruments/sing with three other people.				
QUICHE Make a meat, cheese, or vegetable quiche.				
QUICKSTEP Learn to dance the quickstep.				
QUICK-WITTED Enjoy a keen, alert, ready wit.				
QUIET Arrange to have some peace and quiet.				
QUIZ PROGRAM Match wits with contestants.				
QUOTATIONS Collect wonderful quotations.				
RACKET Play tennis.				

HOW TO ENJOY YOUR RETIREMENT

Topic	Interested?			Remarks
	Yes	No	Later	
RACONTEUR Become a skilled storyteller.				
RAILROAD Collect/trade/sell model trains.				
RAIN GAUGE Keep a weather diary.				
RANCH Visit a dude ranch.				
RANGER Volunteer as a forest ranger.				
RAPIER Learn to duel.				
RASPBERRY Grow raspberries/make preserves.				
RAVIOLI Make some, or order at an Italian restaurant.				
RAZE Tear down that old shed.				
READ Read anything and everything.				
RECIPE Try new recipes; enter contests.				

Topic	Interested?			Remarks
	Yes	No	Later	
RECITAL Attend/give a recital.				
RECLAIM Bring back a vacant lot/ swamp or other area.				
RECONCILE Revive friendship after a quarrel.				
RECREATION Refresh your body/mind.				
RED CROSS Volunteer for the Red Cross.				
RED-HOT Get excited about a new idea.				
RED SNAPPER Catch/cook/eat red snapper.				
REEL Reel in that big fish; dance one, Virginia.				
REFEREE Act as referee for sports events.				
REFRESHER COURSE Take a class at community college.				
REJOIN Reunite with old friends/clubs.				

Topic	Interested?			Remarks
	Yes	No	Later	
REMINISCE Remember the good times.				
REPRESENTATIVE Know what your politicians are doing.				
RESTAURANT Open one if you're a good cook.				
RETREAT Buy/rent one; go on a religious retreat.				
REUNION Plan a family/class/military reunion.				
REVEL Rejoice in your new-found freedom.				
REWARD Feel satisfied with what you do/have/own.				
RICH Beware of get-rich-quick schemes.				
RIFLE Hunt with/collect firearms.				
RINGER Join a group of bell ringers, or play horseshoes.				

Topic	Interested?			Remarks
	Yes	No	Later	
RINSE Cover gray hair with a rinse.				
RIPSAW Work with wood; finish your basement.				
RIVER Take a cruise on a riverboat.				
ROAST Plan a roast for a friend.				
ROBIN Enjoy/feed/study/photograph/ watch birds.				
ROCKING CHAIR You're not ready for one yet.				
ROCKING HORSE Build one for your grand-children.				
SADDLE Take a horseback ride.				
SAILING How about a nice sailboat ride?				
SALMON Grill and serve with cucumber sauce.				

Topic	Interested?			Remarks
	Yes	No	Later	
SALVATION ARMY Work for/donate to the Salvation Army.				
SANTA FE TRAIL Ride the trade route from Independence, MO.				
SAPLING Plant a tree to commemorate a special event.				
SAXOPHONE Learn to play and enjoy.				
SCOUTING Become a leader in the Boy/Girl Scouts.				
SCUBA DIVE Visit colorful fish in lovely warm water.				
SERENDIPITY Notice fortunate discoveries made by accident.				
SHELF Build shelves where needed.				
SHINGLE Check/repair your roof.				
SHIP Take a cruise. Collect/build model ships.				

Topic	Interested?			Remarks
	Yes	No	Later	
SHRUBBERY Trim your shrubs/trees/garden.				
SHUTTLECOCK Play badminton.				
SKYDIVE How about jumping out of an airplane?				
SKYLIGHT Install a skylight; remodel your home.				
SLEUTH Read/write a good mystery.				
SMOKE Quit smoking—again.				
SNOWSHOE Try snowshoeing.				
SOCCER Play/coach soccer.				
SOCRATIC METHOD Learn about this method of instruction.				
SOLDER Make, repair, or connect something metal.				
SONG Sing/write/play a song.				

Topic	Interested?			Remarks
	Yes	No	Later	
SPAY Work to get animals spayed and neutered.				
SPEAR THROWING Enter a spear-throwing contest.				
SPEECH Take a speech class; join Toastmasters.				
SPEEDBOAT Take a ride in a speedboat.				
SPELUNKER Explore/study caves.				
SPORTSWEAR Trade in your business suit.				
SQUEAK Fix squeaks; squeaking wheel gets greased.				
STAINED GLASS Try your hand at this art form.				
STAND-IN Be a stand-in for the star of the show.				
STARGAZE Gaze at/study the stars; daydream.				

Topic	Interested?			Remarks
	Yes	No	Later	
STAR-SPANGLED BANNER Write a new national anthem.				
STATISTICIAN Collect/tabulate statistical data.				
STEPPINGSTONE Place steppingstones in your garden.				
STOCKBROKER Monitor your portfolio closely.				
STOCK CAR Build/race a stock car.				
STONE AGE Study cultural evolution and/or stone implements.				
STOPWATCH Help out as a timer at athletic events.				
STRETCH Do stretching exercises; keep flexible.				
SUICIDE Work a suicide hot line.				
SUNRISE Watch/paint/photograph the sunrise/sunset.				

Topic	Interested?			Remarks
	Yes	No	Later	
SUPERMARKET Share the shopping.				
SUPERNATURAL Study phenomena beyond the known laws of nature.				
SURVEILLANCE Become a brilliant private investigator.				
SURVEY Do a survey in your area.				
SWIM Swim for fun/exercise.				
SWISS Visit Switzerland; open a Swiss bank account.				
TABERNACLE Volunteer at your place of worship.				
TABLE TENNIS Play ping pong.				
TACO Make a Mexican dinner; invite friends.				
TAILOR Make/repair garments.				

Topic	Interested?			Remarks
	Yes	No	Later	
TALENT Use all your talents.				
TALK Talk to everyone you meet.				
TALMUD Study Jewish civil/religious law.				
TANDEM Ride a bicycle built for two.				
TANGO Learn this beautiful Latin dance.				
TAX Prepare taxes for others.				
TAXICAB Drive a taxi in your spare time.				
TAXIDERMY Stuff/mount animals/fish.				
TEDDY BEAR Study the history of/collect teddy bears.				
TEENAGE Work with teens.				
TELEPATHY Study/practice mind communication.				

Topic	Interested?			Remarks
	Yes	No	Later	
TELEPHONE Phone your friends often.				
TIME CLOCK You don't have to punch a time clock now.				
TRACTOR Collect/swap/trade toy farm implements.				
TRAIN Collect toy trains; build layouts.				
TRANSLATE Help someone with foreign languages.				
TRAVEL Travel where you've always wanted to go.				
TRAVELOGUE Speak about/show slides of your trip.				
TRICEPS Exercise with weights.				
TRICYCLE Buy a tricycle for your grandchild.				
TROJAN WAR Study the ten-year war.				

Topic	Interested?			Remarks
	Yes	No	Later	
TROPIC Fly off to the tropics.				
TROPICAL FISH Have a beautiful aquarium.				
TROUT Fish in the mountains.				
TROWEL Learn to lay bricks.				
TUNE-UP Get/give your car a tune-up.				
TURKEY Fix a turkey dinner and invite friends.				
TUTOR Be a tutor to someone.				
TUTU Take kids to ballet lessons/a recital.				
UFO Study unidentified flying objects.				
UKRAINIAN Learn about/visit the Ukraine.				
UKULELE Take lessons on the ukulele.				

Topic	Interested?			Remarks
	Yes	No	Later	
UMBRELLA Buy a new umbrella for your picnic table or golf cart.				
UMPIRE Act as umpire for a ballgame.				
UNDERGROUND RAILROAD Learn about antislavery efforts and advocates.				
UNDERSTUDY Stand in for an actor.				
UNESCO Work for the United Nations Educational, Scientific, and Cultural Organization.				
UNICYCLE Ride a single-wheel vehicle.				
UPHOLSTERY Study covering furniture with fabric; redo your chair/sofa.				
URSA MAJOR/MINOR Study astronomy.				
USHER Usher at your place of worship.				
VACATION Take a vacation. You've earned it.				

Topic	Interested?			Remarks
	Yes	No	Later	
VACCINATE Work to vaccinate children/ pets.				
VENEREAL DISEASE Counsel young people on venereal disease.				
VIETNAM Learn about the history/culture of Vietnam.				
VOCABULARY Improve your vocabulary.				
VOCALIST Sing at services/events/parties.				
VOLUNTEER Volunteer at a school/hospital/ nursing home.				
WALK Walk for fun/exercise.				
WAR GAME Play war games with friends.				
WAR PLANE Build/collect models of war planes.				
WATCHMAKER Repair watches; build clocks.				

Topic	Interested?			Remarks
	Yes	No	Later	
WATERCOLOR Paint with watercolors.				
WATERLOO Learn about Napoleon's defeat.				
WEATHER-STRIP Apply weather stripping around windows/doors.				
WEAVE Learn to weave baskets/paper/cloth.				
WEDGWOOD Collect pottery of white cameo on tinted background.				
WHALE Learn about whales; travel to see them.				
WHEELER-DEALER Become one: buy/sell/trade.				
WHIRLPOOL Get into a hot tub.				
WHISKEY Enjoy a toddy before dinner.				
WHITE HOUSE Learn about its present and past residents and furnishings.				

Topic	Interested?			Remarks
	Yes	No	Later	
WHITTLE Turn scraps of wood into toys/ figures/useful items.				
WHODUNIT Read/write a good mystery.				
WILDERNESS Enjoy being in the wilderness.				
WILD WEST Study the early history of the American West.				
WIND GAUGE Study/record/report weather conditions.				
WINDSOR Learn about the British royal family.				
WITCH DOCTOR Learn about the medical/ spiritual practices of this pro- fessional in some societies.				
WOK Cook with this Chinese pan.				
WOODWIND Play a wind instrument.				
WORK OF ART See works of art; create your own.				

Topic	Interested?			Remarks
	Yes	No	Later	
WORKOUT Maintain physical fitness skills/routine.				
WORKSHOP Create a space where you can work.				
WORLD SERIES Enjoy the World Series.				
WORLD WAR I and II Study the two world wars.				
WRESTLING Teach/coach wrestling; wrestle your worries to the ground.				
XENOGAMY Learn/teach about cross pollination between flowers on different plants.				
XENOPHOBIA Study about fear of strangers or foreigners.				
XEROPHYTE Study plants structurally adapted for life with limited water.				
XYLOGRAPHY Study artistic wood carving.				

Topic	Interested?			Remarks
	Yes	No	Later	
XYLOPHONE Learn to play the xylophone.				
YACHT Buy/rent a yacht for a trip.				
YELLOW Appreciate yellow birds, plants, bushes, trees.				
YEW Plant a yew tree.				
YIDDISH Study the Yiddish language.				
YIN/YANG Study Chinese philosophy.				
YODEL Learn to yodel.				
YOGA Take/teach a yoga class for body and mind.				
YORKSHIRE Make a batter pudding and bake it in meat drippings, then invite a guest to help eat it.				
ZEBRA See a zebra at a zoo.				

Topic	Interested?			Remarks
	Yes	No	Later	
ZEN Pursue enlightenment through meditation.				
ZEPPELIN Study airships manufactured by Count Ferdinand von Zeppelin, circa 1910.				
ZINNIA Plant zinnias in your garden.				
ZIRCONIUM Buy a nice item of zirconium jewelry.				
ZITHER Learn to play a zither; play the Third Man Theme.				
ZODIAC Study the signs of the zodiac.				
ZOIC Study geological eras: Archeozoic, Mesozoic, Paleozoic, and Cenozoic eras.				
ZOOM Make pictures more interesting by zooming in or out with your camera/camcorder.				
ZYMURGY Make and enjoy homemade wine or beer.				

Who Are You?

Name

Ancestors

Countries of origin

> Are you interested in studying your ancestors (genealogy), their countries of origin, or their languages? Do you want to visit these countries?

Living relatives (mother/father, brothers/sisters, uncles/aunts, cousins)

> Do you want to know any relatives better? Would you like to have a family reunion?
>
> Do you want to find/reunite with someone?
>
> Do any relationships need repair? When/how?

Religion/faith

> Are you pleased with your current level of involvement in religious activities/community? If no, what do you want to change? When?

Are you physically active? If so, what sports/activities do you enjoy?

Do you have any hobbies (e.g., stamp collecting, cooking, gardening)? If so, what are they?

Do you enjoy any crafts (e.g., needlecraft, woodworking, tole painting, sewing)? If so, what crafts do you enjoy?

Do you enjoy playing card games and/or board games (e.g., bridge, mah-jongg, Scrabble)? If so, what games do you enjoy?

Do you belong to clubs or fraternal organizations so that you have "buddies" to do things with?

Do you have close friends? Have your friendships been affected or will they be affected by your retirement?

Are you involved in your community? How involved do you want to be?

What Have You Done? What Do You Do Well?

Occupation(s)

Talents, languages, skills

Past successes

If you went to college, what did you like to do?

    Offices held

    Accomplishments

While in high school, what did you like to do?

    Offices held

    Accomplishments

Do you sing, dance, or play an instrument?

Do you enjoy sports? As a spectator or participant? What are the sports you enjoy?

Do you enjoy doing things with your significant other? What are they?

When Will or Did You Retire?

Age

Early retirement?

Retired from what/where?

If you have not already retired, when (date) and at what age will you retire?

Is your significant other working? Retired? Has s/he always been home?

How will your significant other feel about having you home full-time?

Where Will You Live?

Will you stay in your present house/condo/apartment?

Is it paid for? If it is not, how much do you still owe?

Do you want a smaller or larger home?

Is your yard too big, too small, just right?

Do you want to move? Where do you want to move?

Do you mind shoveling snow?

Do you enjoy winter sports such as skiing, skating, hockey?

Do you want to live in a retirement community?

Do you want to spend winters in a warm climate? If yes, in what state?

Do you want to be near or away from your children or grandchildren?

Is travel in your plans?

Have you traveled extensively, a little, or never?

Do you own a motorhome or camper?

Why Are You Retiring?

Are you retiring due to age?

Are you taking early retirement?

Are you "fed up" with working?

Are you retiring due to illness?

Is there another reason for your retirement? If so, what?

Who, if anyone, will rely on you for assistance of some kind after you retire?

Do your parents need help?

Does your brother/sister need help?

Do your children or grandchildren need help?

Is there anyone else relying on you?

How do you feel about retirement? What do you expect it to be?

How Will You Pay for Retirement?

Will you have —

a regular (steady) income?

a retirement check?

Social Security? If not now, when?

investment returns?

Do you *need* to work? Full-time or part-time?

Do you *want* to work? Full-time or part-time?

What are your obligations or debts?

House payment/rent

Car payment

Utilities

Food

Credit cards

Other

Can you live on your retirement income, social security, IRAs, and investments (stocks, bonds, annuities)?

How much more do you need or want?

Do you want to enjoy freedom, leisure, travel?

Do you want to start a business of some kind?

Determining Your Net Worth

Assets

Cash (checking and savings accounts)

Securities (stocks and bonds)

Mutual funds

Receivables (loans made, rebates)

Life insurance cash value

Jewelry, art, and antiques (current market value)

Automobiles (current market value)

Retirement accounts

Pension lump-sum value

Home (current market value)

Other real estate (current market value)

Other assets (collections, furniture, appliances; current market value)

Total

Liabilities

Current bills (rent, telephone, electric, gas)

Credit-card debt

Taxes payable

Auto loans

Installment loans

Home mortgage

Home-equity loan

Student loans

Other liabilities (child care, parent care)

Total

Net Worth

Total Assets minus *Total Liabilities* equals *Net Worth*

APPENDIX B

SPENDING TIME WITH GRANDCHILDREN

Time spent with children can be richly rewarding. We are calling them grandchildren in this book, but they could be nieces, nephews, neighbors, or any children you are lucky enough to be around. You'll enjoy yourself, and the children will have some very special memories of you.

ACTIVITIES

Fun activities might include taking your grandchildren on outings. These do not have to be expensive: visit a library; take a nature walk; go to zoos and museums during times of free or reduced admission. Yearly memberships at nearby attractions are a bargain if you visit often. You can also share your own interests and skills with your grandchildren—anything from fixing cars to birdwatching to playing an instrument or a sport. Teach your grandchildren songs and dances from your native heritage, and cook old country dishes together. Travel with them. Teach older children about money management—saving, budgeting, investing, etc.

> Never help a child with a task at which he feels he can succeed.
>
> —Maria Montessori

Libraries and bookstores offer books full of ideas for activities to do with children, and we'll bet you have a few ideas of your own.

Brain Gym—Do whole-brain exercises with your grandchildren. These fun exercises show that movement and learning can work together. Refer to Appendix C for sample *Brain Gym*® activities.

Classics Illustrated Comics—Introduce your grandchild to *Classics Illustrated* comics. Look online at www.jacklakeproductions.com (for *Classics Illustrated Junior*) and at www.classicscentral.com.

Fun with Science and Nature—Gather up some children and have a ball turning them on to science. Browse around www.sciencenewsforkids.com and www.scienceclub.org. Books by Janice VanCleave (Jossey-Bass; Wiley) include activities for kids ages 4–8 and 9–12 and have special sections to refresh your knowledge of science basics. You can also find her tips in the Science for Fun section at http://school.discovery.com/sciencefaircentral (notice there is no "www"), a Discovery Education website dedicated to making teaching and learning an exciting, rewarding adventure.

Money Management—Turn a common practice such as grocery shopping into a learning activity. Get the free guidebook *Kids, Cash, Plastic, and You* from the Federal Citizen Information Center (1-888-878-3256) or visit www.pueblo.gsa.gov.

Travel with Kids—We suggest the book *Have Kid, Will Travel: 101 Survival Strategies for Vacationing with Babies and Young Children* by Claire Tristram (Andrews McMeel). Check for the following at the library: *Great Adventure Vacations with Your Kids* books by Dorothy Jordan and *Camping with Children* books by Beverly Liston.

BABY-SITTING HELP

Choking Hazards—Balloons are the single most dangerous, nonfood choking item for children under three and as old as eleven. Also watch out for marbles, for coins, and for toys with small detachable parts. Any object that can pass through a toilet-paper tube is too small for a child under three to play with. Window treatment and drapery cords also present a choking hazard. You can convert two-corded mini-blinds and wood blinds purchased before 2001 to safer models by contacting 3-Day Blinds (1-800-590-7467, www.3day.com) for a free Child Safety Kit.

Sudden Infant Death Syndrome (SIDS) — Studies have shown that placing a baby to sleep on its back is safer than laying it on its stomach.

Stimulate a Baby's Brain — Be warm, loving, and responsive to the child. Help build attachments. Talk, read, and sing to the child. Establish rituals and routines. Encourage safe exploration and play. Make television viewing selective. Use discipline calmly and as an opportunity to teach. Recognize that each child is unique and grows at an individual rate.

Car Safety — Place car seats in the back seat to avoid airbag injuries to children. No children should ever ride in the front seat of a car with airbags. The middle of the back seat is the safest place for a child to ride.

EDUCATING CHILDREN

If you plan to help children with schoolwork, to get involved with their education, or to volunteer in a classroom, the following information and resources could be useful. The information below is excerpted from "Each child learns in a different way, educators finding" by Carol Kreck, an article that appeared in the *Denver Post*, 1 September 1994, and is still useful today.

> The book *Hassle-Free Homework*, written by Faith Clark and Cecil Clark (Main Street Books), explains how children learn in different ways. Certain characteristics indicate different learning modes, styles, or strengths, as described below.
>
> • **Visual External:** Sensitive to visual environment; learns by watching; likes movies and museums; is good at arranging objects, keeps the room straight.
> • **Visual Internal:** Makes pictures in head; recalls how things look; likes descriptive novels.

- **Auditory External:** Learns by listening; can listen to two conversations at once; especially sensitive to sound; sorts by how things sound.

- **Auditory Internal:** Hears words in head; recalls melodies; talks things over with self; recalls sounds of different voices.

- **Kinesthetic External:** Likes dancing, sports; likes to use hands; learns by doing.

- **Kinesthetic Internal:** Sorts by feelings; has strong body reactions to experiences; learns only when physically comfortable.

Harvard professor Howard Gardner discusses the theory of multiple intelligences in his books *Frames of Mind* (Basic Books) and *The Unschooled Mind* (Basic Books). He names seven intelligences, as follows:

- **Logical/Mathematical:** The ability to handle chains of reasoning and to recognize patterns. Typical of philosophers, mathematicians, scientists.

- **Linguistic:** Sensitivity to the meaning and order of words. Typical of poets, translators, historians, comedians, public speakers.

- **Musical:** The ability to produce and appreciate rhythm, melody, pitch, and tone. Typical of composers, singers.

- **Spatial:** The ability to perceive the visual world accurately and to recreate or modify aspects of that world. Typical of sculptors, architects, artists, surveyors.

- **Bodily/Kinesthetic:** The ability to control one's body movements and to handle objects skillfully. Typical of athletes, dancers, surgeons.

- **Interpersonal:** The ability to discern and respond appropriately to the temperaments and motivations of other people. Typical of politicians, teachers, salespersons, religious leaders, entrepreneurs.

- **Intrapersonal:** The ability to access one's own strengths, weaknesses, desires, and intelligences as a means to understand oneself and others. Typical of psychologists, therapists, social workers.

Bernice McCarthy of Excel, Inc., in Oak Brook, Illinois, developed a method for grouping students according to four learning styles.

- **Innovative Learners:** Seek meaning; need to be personally involved; learn by listening and sharing ideas; interested in people and culture; divergent thinkers who excel in viewing concrete situations from many perspectives; favorite question—"Why/Why not?"; learn by sensing, feeling, and watching. (Likely to excel in counseling, humanities, organizational development.)

- **Analytic Learners:** Seek facts; need to know what the experts think; less interested in people than in concepts; enjoy traditional classrooms; favorite question—"What?"; learn by watching and thinking. (Likely to excel in basic sciences, math, research, planning.)

- **Common Sense Learners:** Need to know how things work; learn by testing theories in ways that seem reasonable; have limited tolerance for "fuzzy ideas"; need hands-on experience; favorite question—"How does this work?"; learn by thinking and doing. (Likely to exceed in engineering, physical sciences, nursing, technical support positions.)

- **Dynamic Learners:** Seek hidden possibilities; learn by trial and error; adaptable to change; function by acting and testing experience; favorite question—"What can this become?"; learn by doing, sensing, and feeling. (Likely to exceed in marketing, sales, action-oriented managerial jobs.)

Adam Robinson is the author of several books on education. You may want to read one or more of them. His titles include *What Smart Students Know* (Three Rivers), *Word Smart II: How to Build a More Powerful Vocabulary, Second Edition* (Princeton Review), and with Martz or Lurie and others *Cracking the GMAT, . . . the GRE, . . . the PSAT, . . . the SAT*, and so on (Princeton Review).

APPENDIX C

. . . .

BRAIN GYM® ACTIVITIES

Brain Gym® is a registered trademark of the Educational Kinesiology Foundation, Ventura, California (1-888-388-9898).

This appendix contains five sample activities from the book *Brain Gym Teacher's Edition*. *Brain Gym* exercises can be applied to any academic skill; visual, mental, or physical task; or performance activity. They are designed to draw out the learner's innate gifts and talents, to reduce stresses and disabilities, and to bring about whole-brain learning. *Brain Gym* can be used by people of all ages. Give it a try. You may want to buy one of the books listed at the end of this paragraph or contact *Brain Gym*'s headquarters for the name of an approved instructor or consultant near you. The books are written by Dr. Paul E. Dennison and Gail E. Dennison, directors of the Educational Kinesiology Foundation. Write to Edu-Kinesthetics, Inc., P.O. Box 3395, Ventura, CA 93006-3395; call 1-888-388-9898; or visit www.braingym.com.

Arm Activation

ILLUSTRATION © LENICE STROHMEIER

Arm Activation is an isometric self-help activity that lengthens the muscles of the upper chest and shoulders. Muscular control for both gross-motor and fine-motor activities originates in this area. If these muscles are shortened from tension, activities related to writing and the control of tools are inhibited.

Teaching Tips

• The student experiences her arms as they hang loosely at her sides.

• The student activates one arm as illustrated [on previous page], while keeping her head relaxed. She then compares the two arms in terms of length, relaxation, and flexibility before activating the other arm.

• Activation is done in four positions: away from the head, forward, backward, and toward the ear.

• The student may feel the arm activation all the way down to the rib cage.

• The student exhales on the activation, releasing the breath over eight or more counts.

• The student may notice increased relaxation, coordination, and vitality as arm tension is released.

• On completing the movement, the student rolls or shakes her shoulders, noticing the relaxation.

Variations

• Take more than one complete breath in each position of activation.

• While activating, reach up to further open the diaphragm.

• This can be done sitting, standing, or lying down.

• Arm Activations can be done in different arm positions (e.g., arm straight ahead, next to hip, behind the waist).

Activates the Brain For

• expressive speech and language ability

• relaxed use of diaphragm and increased respiration

• eye-hand coordination and the manipulation of tools

Academic Skills

• penmanship and cursive writing

• spelling

• creating writing

Related Skills

• operating machines (e.g., a word processor)

Brain Gym® is a registered trademark of the Educational Kinesiology Foundation, Ventura, California (1-888-388-9898).

Behavioral/Postural Correlates

• an increased attention span for written work

• improved focus and concentration without overfocus

• improved breathing and a relaxed attitude

• an enhanced ability to express ideas

• increased energy in hands and fingers (relaxes writer's cramp)

Balance Buttons

ILLUSTRATION © LENICE STROHMEIER

The Balance Buttons provide a quick balance for all three dimensions: left/right, top/bottom, and back/front. Restoring balance to the occiput [the back part of the head] and the inner-ear area helps to normalize the whole body. The student holds the Balance Buttons, located just above the indentation where the skull rests over the neck (about one and one-half to two inches to each side of the back midline) and just behind the mastoid area.

Teaching Tips

• The student holds one Balance Button while holding the navel with the other hand for about thirty seconds, then changes hands to hold the other Balance Button. The chin is tucked in; the head is level.

• Use two or more fingers to assure that the point is covered.

• Some people may experience a pulsation when the point is stimulated or held.

Variations

• Do the activity while standing, sitting, or lying down.

- Stimulate the points by massage before holding them.
- While holding the points, draw circles around a distant object with your nose, move your head from side to side, or look all around you, relaxing both eye and neck muscles.
- Press your head gently back into your fingers while holding the points, releasing neck tension or headache.

Activates the Brain For

- alertness and focus by stimulating the semicircular canals and reticular system
- decision-making, concentrating, and associative thinking
- changing visual focus from point to point
- increased proprioception [receptivity] for balance and equilibrium
- relaxed jaw and cranial movement

Academic Skills

- comprehension for "reading between the lines"
- perception of the author's point of view
- critical judgment and decision-making
- recognition skills for spelling and math

Related Skills

- report writing, reference work, phone or computer work
- release of motion sickness or of ear pressure built up at altitudes

Behavioral/Postural Correlates

- a sense of well-being
- an open and receptive attitude
- eyes, ears, and head more level on shoulders
- relaxation of an overfocused posture or attitude
- improved reflexes, including Cross Crawl ability

Brain Gym® is a registered trademark of the Educational Kinesiology Foundation, Ventura, California (1-888-388-9898).

Hook-Ups

ILLUSTRATION © LENICE STROHMEIER

Hook-ups connect the electrical circuits in the body, containing and thus focusing both attention and disorganized energy. The mind and body relax as energy circulates through areas blocked by tension. The figure 8 pattern of the arms and legs (Part One) follows the energy flow lines of the body. The touching of the fingertips (Part Two) balances and connects the two brain hemispheres.

Brain Gym® is a registered trademark of the Educational Kinesiology Foundation, Ventura, California (1-888-388-9898).

Teaching Tips

• Part One: Sitting, the student crosses the left ankle over the right. He extends his arms before him, crossing the left wrist over the right. He then interlaces his fingers and draws his hands up toward his chest. He may now close his eyes, breathe deeply, and relax for about a minute. Optional: He presses his tongue flat against the roof of his mouth on inhalation, and relaxes the tongue on exhalation.

• Part Two: When ready, the student uncrosses his legs. He touches the fingertips of both hands together, continuing to breathe deeply for about another minute.

Variations

• Hook-ups may also be done while standing.

• Cook's Hook-ups, Part One: The student sits resting his left ankle on his right knee. He grasps his left ankle with his right hand, putting his left hand around the ball of the left foot (or shoe). He breathes deeply for about a minute, then continues with Part Two, as above.

• For Part One of any of the above versions, some people may prefer to place the right ankle and right wrist on top.

Activates the Brain For

• emotional centering

• grounding

• increased attention (stimulates reticular formation)

• cranial movement

Academic Skills

• clear listening and speaking

• test-taking and similar challenges

• work at the keyboard

Behavioral/Postural Correlates

• improved self-control and sense of boundaries

• improved balance and coordination

• increased comfort in the environment (less hypersensitivity)

• deeper respiration

The Owl

ILLUSTRATION © LENICE STROHMEIER

The bird for which this movement is named has a large head, large eyes, and soft feathers that enable it to fly noiselessly. The owl turns its head and eyes at the same time, and has an extremely full range of vision, as it can turn its head over 180 degrees. It also has radar-like hearing. The Owl movement addresses these same visual, auditory, and head-turning skills. The movement releases neck and shoulder tension that develops under stress, especially when

Brain Gym® is a registered trademark of the Educational Kinesiology Foundation, Ventura, California (1-888-388-9898).

Brain Gym® is a registered trademark of the Educational Kinesiology Foundation, Ventura, California (1-888-388-9898).

holding a heavy book or when coordinating the eyes for reading or other near-point skills. Further, the Owl releases neck tension caused by subvocalization while reading. It lengthens neck and shoulder muscles, restoring range of motion and circulation of blood to the brain for improved focus, attention, and memory skills.

Teaching Tips

• The student squeezes one shoulder to release neck muscles tensed in reaction to listening, speaking, or thinking.

• The student moves his head smoothly across the midfield, to the left, then the right, keeping his chin level.

• The student exhales in each extended head position: to the left and then to the right, and again with the head tilted forward, to release back-of-the-neck muscles. The Owl is repeated with the other shoulder.

• The head may move further into the left and right auditory positions with each release.

Variations

• While doing the Owl, blink lightly, allowing eye movement to shift along the horizon.

• Add one or two complete breathing cycles in each of the three extended head positions, relaxing fully.

• Emphasize listening with the left ear (head left), right ear (head right), and both ears together (chin down).

• Make a sound (e.g., the owl's "who-o-o") on exhalation.

Activates the Brain For

• crossing the "auditory midline" (auditory attention, perception, and memory)

• listening to the sound of one's own voice

• short- and long-term memory

• silent speech and thinking ability

• efficient saccadic eye movement [the type used when reading]

• integration of vision and listening with whole-body movement

Academic Skills

- listening comprehension
- speech or oral reports
- mathematical computation
- memory (for spelling or digit spans)
- computer or other keyboard work

Behavioral/Postural Correlates

- the ability to turn the head left and right
- strength and balance of front and back neck muscles
- alleviated squinting or staring habits
- relaxed neck, jaw, and shoulder muscles, even when focusing
- head centering (helps release the need to tilt the head or lean on the elbows)
- balance front- and back-of-the-neck muscles (alleviates overfocused posture)

The Thinking Cap

This activity helps the student focus attention on his hearing. It also relaxes tension in the cranial bones. The student uses his thumbs and

index fingers to pull the ears gently back and unroll them. He begins at the top of the ear and gently massages down and around the curve, ending with the bottom lobe.

Teaching Tips

- The student keeps his head upright, chin comfortably level.
- The process may be repeated three or more times.

ILLUSTRATION © LENICE STROHMEIER

Brain Gym® is a registered trademark of the Educational Kinesiology Foundation, Ventura, California (1-888-388-9898).

Brain Gym® is a registered trademark of the Educational Kinesiology Foundation, Ventura, California (1-888-388-9898).

Variations

- Include sounds (e.g., yawning sounds or vowel sounds).
- Do the movement while looking over a spelling list.

Activates the Brain For

- crossing the auditory midline (including auditory recognition, attention, discrimination, perception, memory)
- listening to one's own speaking voice
- short-term working memory
- silent speech and thinking skills
- increased mental and physical fitness
- hearing with both ears together
- switched-on reticular formation (screens out distracting sounds from relevant ones)

Academic Skills

- listening comprehension
- public speaking, singing, playing a musical instrument
- inner speech and verbal mediation
- spelling (decoding and encoding)

Related Skills

- mental arithmetic
- concentration while working with a computer or other electronic device

Behavioral/Postural Correlates

- improved breathing and energy
- increased voice resonance
- relaxed jaw, tongue, and facial muscles
- improved left-and-right head-turning ability
- enhanced focusing of the attention
- improved equilibrium, especially in a moving vehicle
- a better range of hearing
- expanded peripheral vision

APPENDIX D

· ·

STARTING A BUSINESS:

SOURCES OF HELP AND INFORMATION

If you are planning to start a small business in the United States, the best source of free help and information is the Small Business Administration (SBA). The SBA is a small, independent, federal agency created to assist and counsel U.S. small businesses.

The Small Business Administration

The SBA has regional and district offices throughout the country, so look in your telephone book to see if there is an office in your town. Each SBA office provides free one-on-one counseling through its Service Corps of Retired Executives (SCORE). The SBA offers a "Starter Kit," a publication called *How the SBA Can Help You Go into Business*, and a list of other publications (many of which are free). Call SCORE at 1-800-634-0245, or write to this address:

> U.S. Small Business Administration
> 409 Third Street SW
> Washington, DC 20416

You will find a lot of helpful information regarding the Small Business Administration at the following websites:

> www.sba.gov
>
> www.score.org

For-a-fee booklets are available to cover a wide range of business subjects. Get the list from the SBA, then order the ones you want by writing to this address or visiting the website:

> Superintendent of Documents
> U.S. Government Printing Office
> Washington, DC 20402-9328
>> Website: www.gpoaccess.gov

The Superintendent of Documents also makes available a directory of SBA programs and activities. This lists every program and activity, by office, in the SBA.

The Federal Citizen Information Center in Pueblo, CO (address below) offers many booklets and pamphlets, available at no cost or for a moderate sum. Many of these publications are aimed at people starting a business. They are full of tips and tables to help you sort through business legalities, estimate costs, track expenses, and learn about bookkeeping, budget analysis, marketing, inventory, management, and much more. For all of this information, call 1-888-878-3256, write to the address below, or visit the website listed:

> Federal Citizen Information Center
> Dept. WWW
> Pueblo, CO 81009
>> Website: www.pueblo.gsa.gov

The United States Department of Commerce's "Roadmap" Program provides assistance to small- and medium-sized companies by connecting them to programs and services within all federal agencies. Information is available on federal procurement, exporting, funding sources, franchising, product standards, industry data, and many other subjects.

Contact:

> Roadmap, Office of Business Liaison
> 14th Street and Constitution Ave. NW, Room 5898-C
> U.S. Department of Commerce
> Washington, DC 20230

If your business will be doing anything with food, following are some helpful publications. Also, be sure to check with your own state department of agriculture.

> *Requirements of Laws and Regulations Enforced by the U.S. Food and Drug Administration.* This booklet is available from U.S. Food and Drug Administration, Health and Human Services Department, 5600 Fishers Lane, Rockville, MD 20857 (1-888-463-6332, www.fda.gov).

> *The Safe Food Book: Your Kitchen Guide.* A single copy is free from the Federal Citizen Information Center (address listed previously). Another booklet called *Recipes for Quantity Food Service* is available from the Superintendent of Documents (address listed previously).

Small Business Development Centers

Small Business Development Centers (SBDCs) are excellent sources of help and information to a person just starting out. They can offer business plans, marketing aids, bookkeeping consultations, computer assistance, managerial and technical training, and assessment testing, among other services. SBDCs are usually located at major state universities and sometimes at private colleges.

As we mentioned earlier, volunteering can be a very rewarding and enriching experience. You'll find that this isn't just busy work; rather, volunteering enables you to make wonderful use of your time and talents and may reward you with social and spiritual benefits. The places and ways in which you can volunteer are far too numerous for us to list, but following are a few places to begin. Check your phone book for local chapters of national organizations. You can volunteer in person, join any of these organizations, or send donations. All will be appreciated. At the end of this section, we list books you can refer to for further information regarding volunteering.

Some Places to Volunteer

American Cancer Society
American Legion
AMERICORPS
AMVETS
Big Brothers/Big Sisters of America
Boy Scouts/Girl Scouts of America
Boys and Girls Clubs
Campfire Boys and Girls
Chamber of Commerce
Charity of your choice
Elks Club

For today and its blessings, I owe the world an attitude of gratitude.

—Clarence E. Hodges

Fire departments
Food banks
Goodwill
Governor's office
Greenpeace
Hospitals
Junior League
Keep America Beautiful
Key Club
Kiwanis Club
Knights of Columbus
League of Latin American Citizens
Libraries
Lions Club
Lutheran Brotherhood
Make a Wish Foundation
Mayor's Office
National 4-H Council
Place of worship
Police stations
Prisons
Red Cross
Rotary Club
Royal Neighbors of America
Salvation Army
Schools
Slovene National Benefit Society
State and National Park Services
Telephone Pioneers
U.S. Army and Air Force
U.S. Navy

It's easy to make a buck. It's a lot tougher to make a difference.

—Tom Brokaw

United Business Owners of America
United Way
Veterans of Foreign Wars
Youth Volunteer Corp.

Some Activities to Volunteer

Adopt a grandmother or grandfather at a home for the elderly.

Adopt a school with your friends and tutor the students.

Ask an agency what it needs, and do all you can to provide it.

Build shelves or provide/prepare food at a food bank.

Clean a beach, park, river, or highway.

Clean out your attic and donate clothing and goods to a shelter.

Deliver food to AIDS, elderly, or homebound patients.

Fulfill a wish for a needy family.

Hold an educational seminar for teenage moms.

Mentor an at-risk teen.

Paint over graffiti.

Plant flowers in public places.

Practice job interviews with teens and challenged adults.

Read to a needy child or to an elderly or homebound person.

Recycle fee-deposit items and give the cash to a worthy cause.

Serve lunch at a soup kitchen.

Tape-record books for learning disabled children or blind people.

Teach a child or group of children about something you love.

Teach someone to read.

Visit a veteran's home and share stories or play games.

What else can you do to help?

Volunteering Opportunities That May Take You Around the World

CEDAM International
(for underwater enthusiasts — check on their need for volunteers, which varies year to year)
Reef Environmental Education Foundation (REEF)
(recommended by CEDAM for diving trips that support data collection)

CEDAM International	REEF
One Fox Road	P.O. Box 246
Croton-on Hudson, NY 10520	Key Largo, FL 33037
Website: www.cedam.org	Phone: 1-305-852-0030
	Website: www.reef.org

Founded in 1967, CEDAM International is involved in **C**onservation, **E**ducation, **D**iving, **A**rchaeology, and **M**useum work. They welcome novice and experienced divers, explorers, underwater videographers and photographers as well as amateur and skilled naturalists and marine biologists. CEDAM volunteers bring back live fish for public aquariums. Their website recommends that you check out REEF, which invites you to participate in the Reef Fish Survey Project or to take "dive vacations that count."

Earthwatch
(no special skills required)

3 Clock Tower Place, Suite 100
P.O. Box 75
Maynard, MA 01754
Phone: 1-978-461-0081 or 1-800-776-0188
Website: www.earthwatch.org

Founded in 1971, Earthwatch is the world's largest organization matching members of the public with scientific and conservation projects worldwide. You can be at any fitness level, choose to stay in hotels or to sleep on the ground, and possibly share cooking. Most teams have six to ten people. Outings last ten days to two weeks. Earthwatch wants people who are brimming with curiosity and commitment and who are willing to roll up their sleeves.

> *It is our task in our time and in our generation to hand down undiminished to those who come after us, as was handed down to us by those who went before, the natural wealth and beauty which is ours.*
>
> —John F. Kennedy

Global Volunteers

(no special skills required)

> 375 East Little Canada Road
> St. Paul, MN 55117
> > Phone: 1-800-487-1074
> > Website: www.globalvolunteers.org

Global Volunteers enables people like you to assist others around the world and, in the process, to significantly enhance your own life. You may teach conversational English to elementary, secondary, college, or adult students in classrooms or in small groups. You may build, repair, or paint facilities. Men and women of all ages and backgrounds can help with these projects.

Health Volunteers Overseas

(physicians, dentists, physical therapists, nurses, and other health professionals)

Health Volunteers Overseas
1900 L Street NW, Suite 300
Washington, DC 20036
Phone: 1-202-296-0928
Website: www.hvousa.org

Health Volunteers Overseas is a private nonprofit organization committed to improving health care in developing countries. Volunteers teach as well as provide a professional health service.

Medical Ministry International
(health professionals and fix-it people)

MMI-USA
P.O. Box 1339
Allen, TX 75013
Phone: 1-972-727-5864
Website: www.mmint.org

MGM-Canada, Inc.
15 John Street North, Suite 301
Hamilton, Ontario L8R 1H1
Phone: 1-905-524-3544
Website: www.mmint.org

Medical Ministry International (in Canada the ministry is called Medical Ministry Canada) has a forty-year history of providing opportunities for volunteers to work in one- or two-week medical, dental, surgical, or eye clinics, helping people who have little or no access to medical care. They see over 250,000 patients in over twenty countries annually. This group is interdenominational, serving the poor in the name of Jesus. For more project information about needs for medicines, eyeglasses, computers, vehicles, and additional wish-list items, contact the above addresses.

Travel Agencies

Grand Circle Travel
Phone: 1-800-959-0405
Website: www.gct.com

Grandtravel
(tours for grandparents and school-age grandchildren; also includes aunts and uncles)
Grandtravel, A Division of Academic Travel Abroad, Inc.
1920 N Street NW, Suite 200
Washington, DC 20036
Phone: 1-800-247-7651
Website: www.grandtrvl.com

Mayflower Tours
(escorts local and national travelers to destinations throughout the U.S. and the world. By handling arrangements for individuals and groups who prefer the advantages of escorted travel, Mayflower takes the hassle out of planning a vacation. Mayflower Tours is a member of the United States Tour Operations Association and the National Tour Association, offering adequate protection plans.
1225 Warren Avenue
Downers Grove, IL 60515
Phone: 1-800-323-7604 or 1-630-435-8500
Website: www.mayflowertours.com

. . . .

Saga Holidays, Ltd.
("If you're over 50, you've chosen the perfect travel partner.")
The Saga Building, Enbrook Park, Folkestone
Kent CT20 3SE, England
Phone (overseas call) +44 1303 771190
Website: www.sagaholidays.com

Airlines

The airlines sell coupon books to people over age sixty-two (some younger). Certain restrictions apply regarding advance purchase, days of travel, etc. Special rates often apply to travel companions. Check with the individual airlines about their senior citizen travel clubs. Also ask if you are getting the cheapest fare available. Check the Yellow Pages for the local numbers of national and foreign carriers.

National Airlines

America West & U.S. Airways	1-800-235-9292 www.americawest.com
American	1-800-433-7300 www.aa.com
Continental	1-800-523-3273 www.continental.com
Delta	1-800-241-4141 www.delta.com
Northwest	1-800-225-2525 www.nwa.com
Southwest Airlines	1-800-435-9792 www.southwest.com
United	1-800-241-6522 www.ual.com

Foreign Airlines

Aer Lingus (Ireland)	1-800-474-7424
	www.aerlingus.com
Air Canada	1-888-247-2262
	www.aircanada.com
British Airways	1-800-247-9297
	www.britishairways.com
China	1-800-227-5118
	www.china-airlines.com
KLM Royal Dutch (partnered in U.S. with Northwest Airlines)	1-800-374-7747 www.klm.com
Lufthansa	1-800-645-3880
	www.lufthansa.com
Mexicana	1-800-531-7921
	www.mexicana.com
SAS (Scandinavian)	1-800-221-2350
	www.scandinavian.net

Car Rental

Discounts are available to members of various senior citizen groups, e.g., AARP, airline and travel clubs, and hotel travel clubs. Ask about discounts when you make your reservation.

Alamo	1-800-462-5266
	www.goalamo.com
Avis	1-800-230-4898
	www.avis.com

Budget	1-800-527-0700
	www.budgetrentacar.com
Dollar	1-800-800-3665
	www.dollarcar.com
Hertz	1-800-654-3131
	www.hertz.com
National	1-800-227-7368
	www.nationalcar.com
Thrifty	1-800-367-2277
	www.thrifty.com

Cruise Lines

Carnival	1-800-227-6425
	www.carnival.com
Cruise One	1-800-532-7447
	www.cruiseone.com
Cunard	1-800-221-4770
	www.cunardline.com
Holland America	1-800-426-0327
	www.hollandamerica.com
Norwegian	1-800-262-4625
	www.ncl.com
Royal Caribbean	1-866-562-7625
	www.royalcaribbean.com

Hotels

Check your Yellow Pages for the following hotels' local phone numbers or different toll-free numbers if those given below do not work in your area. (Some toll-free-number companies only want to pay the charges for a certain state or a certain area. Others will accept charges from the whole United States.) Following are some questions to ask:

1. What organizations are entitled to discounts? (AARP, airline clubs, travel clubs, etc.)
2. Are there restrictions regarding age of traveler and age of companion?
3. What is the percent of discount?
4. What is the cost to join the hotel's own travel club or program?
5. Do traveling companions or grandchildren under age eighteen stay free?
6. Is there a free breakfast or discounted food? free newspaper, long distance calls, coffee or tea? a happy hour?
7. Must you reserve for yourself or through a travel agent?
8. What are the regions or states where this hotel chain operates?
9. Are there blackout periods or restrictions on days of the week, length of stay, or holiday stays?

Offers can change from time to time, so be sure to check what is current. Call or write ahead for a directory and information.

Best Western International
  1-800-780-7234
www.bestwestern.com
Gold Crown Club® International

Choice Hotels International
  1-877-424-6423
www.choicehotels.com
Easy Choice or Choice Privileges®

Comfort Inns and Suites
  1-800-228-5150
www.comfortinn.com
Choice Privileges®

Days Inns
  1-800-329-7466
www.daysinn.com
Trip Rewards

Doubletree Club Hotels
  1-800-222-8733
www.doubletreehotels.com
Hilton HHonors

Drury Inns	www.drury-inn.com
1-800-378-7966	*Gold Key Club*
EconoLodge	www.econolodge.com
1-800-553-2666	*Easy Choice*
Embassy Suites	www.embassysuites.com
1-800-362-2779	*Hilton HHonors*
Hampton Inns	www.hamptoninn.com
1-800-426-7866	*Hilton HHonors*
Hilton Hotels	www.hilton.com
1-800-445-8667	*Hilton HHonors*
Holiday Inns	www.ichotelsgroup.com
1-800-465-4329	*Priority Club®*
Howard Johnson's Motor Lodges	www.hojo.com
1-800-446-4656	*TripRewards®*
Hyatt Hotels and Resorts	www.hyatt.com
1-888-591-1234	*Gold Passport®*
Inn Suites (in AZ and CA)	www.innsuites.com
1-800-842-4242	*InnSuites Inn Club*
Knights Inns	www.knightsinn.com
1-800-843-5644	*TripRewards®*
La Quinta Inns	www.lq.com
1-866-725-1661	*senior discounts*
Marriott Hotels & Resorts	www.marriott.com
1-888-236-2427	*Marriott Rewards*
Quality Inns	www.choicehotels.com
1-877-424-6423	*Choice Privileges®*
Radisson Hotels & Resorts	www.radisson.com
1-888-201-1718	*Gold Points*
Ramada Worldwide	www.ramada.com
1-800-272-6232	*TripRewards®*
Red Roof Inns	www.redroof.com
1-800-733-7663	*RediCard®*

Renaissance Hotels & Resorts
     1-800-468-3571

www.marriott.com/
renaissancehotels
Marriott Rewards

Rodeway Inns
     1-877-424-6423

www.choicehotels.com
Easy Choice

Sheraton Hotels
     1-800-598-1753

www.starwoodhotels.com/
sheraton
Starwood Preferred Guest®

Shoney's Inns (mostly in southeast)
     1-800-552-4667

www.shoneysinn.com
senior discounts

Sonesta Worldwide
     1-800-766-3782

www.sonesta.com
senior discounts

Travelodge
     1-800-578-7878

www.travelodge.com
TripRewards®

Westin Hotels & Resorts
     1-800-937-8461

www.starwoodhotels.com/
westin
Starwood Preferred Guest®

Vacation Rental Homes

At Home Abroad
     1-212-421-9165

www.athomeabroadinc.com

Interhome
     1-800-882-6864

www.interhome.com

RentaVilla.com
     1-800-964-1891

www.rentavilla.com

Vacation Rental Managers
Association
     1-831-426-8762

www.vrma.com

Vacation Villas International
     (Germany)
     +49 01561 920 950 10

www.vacationvillas.net

Contact Information for State and Local Visitors Bureaus

Alabama

Alabama Bureau of Tourism and Travel
401 Adams Avenue
P.O. Box 4927
Montgomery, AL 36103
Phone: 1-334-242-4169
or 1-800-ALA-BAMA (252-2262)
Travel Website: www.touralabama.org

Alaska

Alaska Division of Tourism
P.O. Box 110801
Juneau, AK 99811
Phone: 1-907-929-2200 or 1-800-327-9372
Travel Website: www.travelalaska.com

Arizona

Arizona Office of Tourism
2702 North 3rd Street
Phoenix, AZ 85004
Phone: 1-866-275-5816
Travel Website: www.arizonaguide.com

Arkansas

Department of Parks and Tourism
One Capitol Mall
Little Rock, AR 72201
Phone: 1-501-682-7777
or 1-800-NATURAL (628-8725)
Travel Website: www.arkansas.com

California

California Tourism
P.O. Box 1499
Sacramento, CA 95812
Phone: 1-916-444-4429
or 1-800-862-2543
Travel Website: www.gocalif.ca.gov

Colorado

Colorado Tourism Office
1625 Broadway, Suite 1700
Denver, CO 80202
Phone: 1-303-892-3840
or 1-800-COLORADO (265-6723)
Travel Website: www.colorado.com

Denver Metro Convention and Visitors Bureau
1555 California Street, #300
Denver, CO 80202
Phone: 1-303-892-1112
or 1-800-233-6837
Travel Website: www.denver.org

Pueblo Convention and Visitors Council
302 North Santa Fe Avenue
Pueblo, CO 81003
Phone: 1-719-542-1704
or 1-800-233-3446
Travel Website: www.pueblochamber.org

Connecticut

Connecticut State Board of Tourism
Department of Economic Development, Tourism Division
505 Hudson Street
Hartford, CT 06106

Phone: 1-800-CT-BOUND (282-6863)
Travel Website: www.ct.gov

Delaware

Delaware Tourism Office
99 Kings Highway
Dover, DE 19901
Phone: 1-302-739-4271
or 1-866-284-7483
Travel Website: www.delaware.gov

District of Columbia

Washington DC Convention and Tourism Corporation
901 7th Street NW, 4th Floor
Washington, DC 20001
Travel Website: www.washington.org

Florida

Florida State Board of Tourism
P.O. Box 1100
Tallahassee, FL 32302
Phone: 1-888-735-2872
Travel Website: www.visitflorida.com

Georgia

Department of Industry, Trade & Tourism
Peachtree Center Avenue NE, Suites 1000 & 1100
Atlanta, GA 30303
Phone: 1-800-VISIT-GA (847-4842)
Travel Website: www.georgia.gov

Hawaii

Hawaii Visitors & Convention Bureau
2270 Kalakaua Avenue, Suite 801
Honolulu, HI 96815

Phone: 1-800-464-2924

Travel Website: www.gohawaii.com

Idaho

Idaho Dept. of Commerce, Travel, Leisure & Tourism

700 West State Street

Boise, ID 83720

Phone: 1-208-334-2470

or 1-800-VISIT-ID (847-4843)

Travel Website: www.visitidaho.org

Illinois

Illinois Dept. of Commerce & Economic Opportunity

620 East Adams Street

Springfield, IL 62701

Phone: 1-217-782-7500

or 1-800-2CONNECT (406-6418)

Travel Website: www.enjoyillinois.com

Indiana

Indiana Office of Tourism Development

One North Capitol, Suite 100

Indianapolis, IN 46204

Phone: 1-888-ENJOY-IN (365-6946)

Travel Website: www.enjoyindiana.com

Iowa

Iowa Department of Economic Development

200 East Grand Avenue

Des Moines, IA 50309

Phone: 1-515-242-4700

or 1-800-245-IOWA (4692)

Travel Website: www.traveliowa.com

Kansas

Kansas Department of Commerce
1000 SW Jackson Street, Suite 100
Topeka, KS 66612
Phone: 1-785-296-3481
or 1-800-2KANSAS (252-6727)
Travel Website: www.travelks.com

Kentucky

Kentucky Department of Tourism
Capital Plaza Tower, Floor 22
500 Mero Street
Frankfort, KY 40601
Phone: 1-502-564-4930
or 1-800-225-TRIP (225-8747)
Travel Website: www.kentuckytourism.com

Louisiana

Louisiana Office of Tourism
1051 N. Third Street
Baton Rouge, LA 70804
Phone: 1-225-342-8119
or 1-800-33GUMBO (334-8626)
Travel Website: www.louisianatravel.com

Maine

Maine Office of Tourism
59 State House Station
Augusta, ME 04333
Phone: 1-888-624-6345
Travel Website: www.visitmaine.com

Maryland

Maryland Office of Tourism Development
217 East Redwood Street
Baltimore, MD 21202
Phone: 1-877-209-5883
or 1-866-MD-WELCOME (639-3526)
Travel Website: www.mdisfun.org

Massachusetts

Massachusetts Office of Travel and Tourism
10 Park Plaza, Suite 4510
Boston, MA 02116
Phone: 1-617-973-8500
or 1-800-227-MASS (6277)
Travel Website: www.massvacation.com

Michigan

Travel Michigan
300 North Washington Square
Lansing, MI 48913
Phone: 1-800-543-2937
Travel Website: www.michigan.org

Minnesota

Minnesota Office of Tourism
100 Metro Square
121 7th Place East
St. Paul, MN 55101
Phone: 1-651-296-5029
or 1-888-868-7476
Travel Website: www.exploreminnesota.com

Mississippi

Mississippi Division of Tourism Development
P.O. Box 849
Jackson, MS 39205
> Phone: 1-601-359-3449
> > or 1-866-SEE-MISS (733-6477)
> Travel Website: www.visitmississippi.org

Missouri

Missouri Division of Tourism
P.O. Box 1055
Truman State Office Building
Jefferson City, MO 65102
> Phone: 1-573-751-4133
> > or 1-800-519-2100
> Travel Website: www.missouritourism.org

Montana

Montana Department of Commerce
301 S. Park Avenue
Helena, MT 59601
> Phone: 1-406-841-2700
> > or 1-800-VISIT-MT (847-4868)
> Travel Website: www.visitmt.com

Nebraska

Nebraska Division of Travel and Tourism
P.O. Box 98907
Lincoln, NE 68509
> Phone: 1-402-471-3791
> > or 1-877-NEBRASKA (632-7275)
> Travel Website: www.visitnebraska.org

Nevada

Nevada Commission on Tourism
401 N. Carson Street
Carson City, NV 89701
>Phone: 1-800-237-0774
>>or 1-800-NEVADA-8 (638-2328)
>Travel Website: www.travelnevada.com

New Hampshire

New Hampshire Division of Travel & Tourism Development
P.O. Box 1856
Concord, NH 03302
>Phone: 1-603-271-2665 to speak with travel
>>counselors
>>1-800-FUN-IN-NH (386-4664) to obtain kits
>Travel Website: www.visitnh.gov

New Jersey

New Jersey Office of Travel and Tourism
20 West State Street CN820
Trenton, NJ 08625
>Phone: 1-609-777-0885
>>or 1-800-VISIT-NJ (847-4865)
>Travel Website: www.visitnj.org

New Mexico

New Mexico Department of Tourism
491 Old Santa Fe Trail
Santa Fe, NM 87503
>Phone: 1-505-827-7400
>>or 1-800-733-6396
>Travel Website: www.newmexico.org

New York

New York Department of Tourism
P.O. Box 2603
One Commerce Plaza
Albany, NY 12220
    Phone: 1-518-474-4116
        or 1-800-CALL-NYS (225-5697)
    Travel Website: www.iloveny.state.ny.us

North Carolina

North Carolina Department of Commerce
301 North Wilmington Street
Raleigh, NC 27601
    Phone: 1-919-715-5900
        or 1-800-VISIT-NC (847-4862)
    Travel Website: www.visitnc.com

North Dakota

North Dakota Tourism Department
604 East Boulevard
Bismark, ND 58505
    Phone: 1-701-328-2525
        or 1-800-HELLO-ND (435-5663)
    Travel Website: www.ndtourism.com

Ohio

Ohio Department of Commerce
77 South High Street, 23rd Floor
Columbus, OH 43215
    Phone: 1-614-466-8844
        or 1-800-BUCKEYE (282-5393)
    Travel Website: www.discoverohio.com

Oklahoma

Oklahoma Tourism and Recreation Department
120 North Robinson Avenue, 6th Floor
Oklahoma City, OK 73102
Phone: 1-405-230-8400
or 1-800-652-6552
Travel Website: www.oklatourism.gov

Oregon

Oregon Tourism Commission
775 Summer Street, NE
Salem, OR 97301
Phone: 1-503-986-0123
or 1-800-547-7842
Travel Website: www.traveloregon.com

Pennsylvania

Pennsylvania Tourism Office
Commonwealth Keystone Building
400 North Street
Harrisburg, PA 17120
Phone: 1-717-787-5453
or 1-800-VISIT-PA (847-4872)
Travel Website: www.visitpa.com

Rhode Island

Rhode Island Economic Development Corporation
1 West Exchange Street
Providence, RI 02903
Phone: 1-401-222-2601
or 1-800-556-2484
Travel Website: www.visitrhodeisland.com

South Carolina

South Carolina Department of Parks, Recreation,
and Tourism
1205 Pendleton Street, Suite 106
Columbia, SC 29201
Phone: 1-803-734-1700
Travel Website: www.discoversouthcarolina.com

South Dakota

South Dakota Department of Tourism
711 East Wells Avenue
c/o 500 East Capitol Avenue
Pierre, SD 57501
Phone: 1-605-773-3301
or 1-800-S-DAKOTA (732-5682)
Travel Website: www.travelsd.com

Tennessee

Tennessee Department of Tourist Development
312 8th Avenue North, 25th Floor
Nashville, TN 37243
Phone: 1-615-741-2158
or 1-800-GO2-TENN (462-8366)
Travel Website: www.tnvacation.com

Texas

Texas Dept. of Economic Development and Tourism
P.O. Box 12428
Austin, TX 78711
Phone: 1-512-936-0101
or 1-800-8888-TEX (839)
Travel Website: www.traveltex.com

Utah

Utah Office of Tourism
Council Hall, Capitol Hill
300 North State
    Salt Lake City, UT 84114
    Phone: 1-801-538-1900
        or 1-800-200-1160
    Travel Website: www.travel.utah.gov

Vermont

Vermont Department of Tourism & Marketing
6 Baldwin Street, Drawer 33
Montpelier, VT 05633
    Phone: 1-802-828-3676
        or 1-800-VERMONT (837-6668)
    Travel Website: www.vermontvacation.com

Virginia

Virginia Division of Tourism
901 East Byrd Street
Richmond, VA 23919
    Phone: 1-804-786-2051
        or 1-800-VISIT-VA (847-4882)
    Travel Website: www.virginia.org

Washington

Washington State Department of Tourism
P.O. Box 42525
Olympia, WA 98504
    Phone: 1-360-725-4000
        or 1-800-544-1800
    Travel Website: www.experiencewashington.com

West Virginia

West Virginia Division of Tourism
90 MacCorkle Avenue SW
S. Charleston, WV 25303
 Phone: 1-304-558-2200
 or 1-800-CALL-WVA (225-5982)
Travel Website: www.wvtourism.com

Wisconsin

Wisconsin Department of Tourism
201 West Washington Avenue
P.O. Box 8690
Madison, WI 53708
 Phone: 1-608-266-7621
 or 1-800-432-TRIP (8747)
Travel Website: www.travelwisconsin.com

Wyoming

Wyoming Travel & Tourism
I-25 (Interstate 25) at College Drive
Cheyenne, WY 82002
 Phone: 1-307-777-7777
 or 1-800-CALL-WYO (225-5996)
Travel Website: www.wyomingtourism.org

Hiking Information Sources

Continental Divide Trail

Continental Divide Trail Alliance
P.O. Box 628
Pine, CO 80470

Phone: 1-303-838-3760

or 1-888-909-CDTA (2382)

Website: www.cdtrail.org

Greenbrier River Trail

Star Route, Box 125

Caldwell, WV 24925

Phone: 1-800-336-7009 (Pocahontas County)

1-800-833-2068 (Greenbrier County)

Website: www.greenbrierrivertrail.com

Idaho Centennial Trail

Idaho Department of Parks and Recreation

P.O. Box 83720

Boise, ID 83720

Phone: 1-208-334-4180, ext. 228

Website: www.idahoparks.org/recreation/hiking.aspx

Marble Mountain Wilderness

Klamath National Forest

1312 Fairlane Road

Yreka, CA 96097

Phone: 1-530-842-6131

Website: www.fs.fed.us/r5/klamath/recreation/

wilderness/marbles

Mariscal Canyon Rim Trail

Park Superintendent

P.O. Box 129

Big Bend National Park, TX 79834

Phone: 1-432-477-2251

Website: www.nps.gov/bibe/visit/activities/greathikes.

htm#rugged

Also see: www.trails.com/tcatalog_trail.

asp?trailid=HGS168-025

Ozark Trail

Ozark Trail Association
483 South Kirkwood Road, #40
Kirkwood, MO 63122
   Phone: 1-573-786-2065
   Website: www.ozarktrail.com

Smarts Brook Trail

White Mountain National Forest
719 Main Street
Laconia, NH 03246
   Phone: 1-603-528-8721
   Website: www.fs.fed.us/r9/forests/white_mountain/
      recreation/skiing/SmartsBrook.php

Superior Hiking Trail

Superior Hiking Trail Association
P.O. Box 4
Two Harbors, MN 55616
   Phone: 1-218-834-2700
   Website: www.shta.org

Additional Reading and Internet Sites Related to Travel

BOOKS

A Field Guide to the Birds of Eastern and Central North America
by Roger Tory Peterson (Houghton Mifflin)

. . . .

Field Guide to Mysterious Places of Eastern North America
Field Guide to Mysterious Places of the West
Field Guide to Mysterious Places of the Pacific Coast
All by Salvatore M. Trento (Owl Books/Henry Holt). These books give information about enigmatic sites: caves, tunnels, and other places linked to unexplained phenomena.

Fundamentals of Search and Rescue by Donald C. Cooper (Jones & Bartlett)

Gettysburg: A Battlefield Guide (This Hallowed Ground, Guides to Civil War Battlefield Series) by Mark Grimsley and Brooks Simpson (Bison Books Corporation). This book is an excellent guide describing the events of the Battle of Gettysburg.

Mountain Search and Rescue Techniques by Bill May. Written in 1972 (and available on Amazon.com), it is still highly regarded as a great text for search and rescue application. The book offers thorough discussion of topics ranging from knots to missing-person search patterns to technical rock rescues.

Off the Beaten Path: A Guide to More Than 1,000 Scenic and Interesting Places Still Uncrowded and Inviting by Readers Digest. This book lists, state by state, all kinds of little-known places to visit.

Woodall Publishing offers dozens of guides that provide RV, tenting, and campground information for different regions and interests. Call 1-877-680-6155 or visit www.woodalls.com.

CATALOGS

Asia Transpacific Journeys has catalogs and information about trips to Southeast Asia (1-800-642-2742; www.asiatranspacific.com).

Butterfield & Robinson catalog lists biking and walking tours (1-866-551-9090; www.butterfield.com).

Club America has a Vacations Planner that describes holidays all over the world (1-800-221-4969; www.clubamericatravel.com).

ElderTreks catalog specializes in trips for older travelers (1-800-741-7956; www.eldertreks.com).

Interhostel catalog lists international study programs for travelers age fifty and older (1-800-733-9753 or 1-603-862-1147; www.learn.unh.edu/interhostel).

INTERNET

Journeywoman is a website full of tips and information designed to encourage women to travel; website: http://www.journeywoman.com.

National Parks Conservation Association website: http://www.npca.org.

TripSpot.com is a user-friendly place to go surfing for travel ideas and information (www.tripspot.com/state).

APPENDIX G

ADDITIONAL INFORMATION RESOURCES

AGING

Aging Network Services

4400 East-West Highway #907

Bethesda, MD 20814

Phone: 1-301-657-4329

Website: www.agingnets.com

Aging Network Services offers counseling on care management for aging relatives and concerned family members. Call or write for brochures and information on fees.

National Council on the Aging

300 D Street SW, Suite 801

Washington, DC 20024

Phone: 1-202-479-1200 (for catalog of publications)

Website: www.ncoa.org

ALLERGIES

The Gluten-Free Pantry

P.O. Box 840

Glastonbury, CT 06033

Inquiries and Customer Service: 1-860-633-3826

Orders: 1-800-291-8386

Website: www.glutenfree.com

This mail order company sells gluten-free baking mixes for pasta, brownies, muffins, bagels, breads, and more.

ARTHRITIS

Arthritis Foundation

> P.O. Box 7669
> Atlanta, GA 30357
> > Phone: 1-800-568-4045
> > Website: www.arthritis.org

The Arthritis Foundation offers self-help courses, exercise programs, support groups, and pamphlets on arthritis and its management. Check your White Pages for a local chapter or contact the national office.

CANCER

American Cancer Society

> > Phone: 1-800-227-2345
> > Website: www.cancer.org

Prostate Cancer Foundation

> 1250 Fourth Street
> Santa Monica, CA 90401
> > Phone: 1-800-757-CURE (2873)
> > Website: www.prostatecancerfoundation.org

Y-ME National Breast Cancer Organization

> 212 W. Van Buren, Suite 1000
> Chicago, IL 60607
> > Phone: 1-800-221-2141
> > Website: www.y-me.org

24-hour/7-days a week breast cancer support from survivors and supporters. Interpreters available in 150 languages.

CARPAL TUNNEL

Center for Carpal Tunnel Studies

10585 North Tatum Boulevard, Suite D-135

Paradise Valley, AZ 85253

Phone: 1-480-483-7387

Website: www.centerforcarpaltunnel.com

Dr. Benjamin Sucher has a course/workshop and videos for treatment of this painful syndrome.

CHILDREN

Partnership for a Drug-Free America

405 Lexington Avenue, Suite 1601

New York, NY 10174

Phone: 1-212-922-1560

Website: www.drugfree.org

Save the Children Headquarters

54 Wilton Road

Westport, CT 06880

Phone: 1-800-728-3843

or 1-203-221-4030

Website: www.savethechildren.org

Shriners Hospitals for Crippled Children

Phone: 1-800-237-5055

Website: www.shrinershq.org

Shriners Hospitals offer expert orthopedic and burn care for children.

DIABETES

American Diabetes Association

ATTN: National Call Center

1701 North Beauregard Street

Alexandria, VA 22311

Phone: 1-800-DIABETES (342-2383)

Website: www.diabetes.org

The American Diabetes Association offers a wealth of educational literature plus counseling, lectures, and workshops. Check your White Pages for a local listing.

EARS AND EYES

American Speech-Language-Hearing Association

10801 Rockville Pike

Rockville, MD 20852

Phone: 1-800-638-8255 or 1-301-897-5700 (TTY)

Website: www.asha.org

This association offers information on hearing aids, hearing loss, and communication problems. It also provides lists of certified audiologists and speech pathologists in each state.

National Information Center on Deafness

Gallaudet University

800 Florida Avenue, NE

Washington, DC 20002

Phone: 1-202-651-5000 (TTY/Voice)

Website: www.gallaudet.edu

Self Help for Hard of Hearing People, Inc. (SHHH)

7910 Woodmont Avenue, #1200

Bethesda, MD 20814

Phone: 1-301-657-2248

or 1-301-657-2249 (TTY)

Website: www.shhh.org

American Printing House for the Blind

(braille and large-type books)

1839 Frankfort Avenue

P.O. Box 6085

Louisville, KY 40206

Phone: 1-800-223-1839
Website: www.aph.org

Prevent Blindness America

211 West Wacker Drive, Suite 1700
Chicago, IL 60606
Phone: 1-800-331-2020
Website: www.preventblindness.org

This national society offers a variety of materials on eye health and safety, including information on cataracts, diabetic retinopathy, and glaucoma. Also call the **National Center for Sight** at 1-800-221-3004.

ENVIRONMENT

Greenpeace International

(environmental specialists)
702 H Street NW
Washington, DC 20001
Phone: 1-800-326-0959
or 1-202-462-1177
Website: www.greenpeace.org

National Arbor Day Foundation

(trees and tree planting)
100 Arbor Avenue
Nebraska City, NE 68410
Phone: 1-888-448-7337
Website: www.arborday.org

National Audubon Society

(bird specialists)
700 Broadway
New York, NY 10003
Phone: 1-212-979-3000
Website: www.audubon.org

Sierra Club

(trees, wilderness, and environment)

85 Second Street, 2nd Floor
San Francisco, CA 94105
Phone: 1-415-977-5500
Website: www.sierraclub.org

HEAD AND NECK PAIN

American Academy of Otolaryngology

(head and neck surgery)

1 Prince Street
Alexandria, VA 22314
Phone: 1-703-836-4444
Website: www.entnet.org

HEALTH REFERRAL

National Health Information Center

(health referral service)

ODPHP
1101 Wootton Parkway, Suite LL100
Rockville, MD 20852
Phone: 1-240-453-8280
Website: www.odphp.osophs.dhhs.gov/pubs

ODPHP stands for Office of Disease Prevention and Health Promotion. This office will refer you to organizations that can respond to your specific health questions.

HEART HEALTH

American Heart Association

7272 Greenville Avenue
Dallas, TX 75231
Phone: 1-800-AHA-USA-1 (242-8721)
Website: www.americanheart.org

The American Heart Association offers books and information regarding heart attack prevention and rehabilitation. Check your White Pages for a local listing, or visit their website.

LUNG HEALTH

American Lung Association

> 61 Broadway, 6th Floor
> New York, NY 10006
> > Phone: 1-800-548-8252
> > Website: www.lungusa.org

They do have information regarding flu and smoking cessation.

MEDICINE

National Council on Patient Information and Education

> 4915 Saint Elmo Avenue, Suite 505
> Bethesda, MD 20814
> > Phone: 1-301-656-8565
> > Website: www.talkaboutrx.org

Order your 7-item "Talk About Prescriptions" pack. Send $2.00 and a self-addressed, business-size (#10) envelope to TAP-PAK, c/o NCPIE at the address above.

MENTAL HEALTH

Alzheimer's Association

> 225 North Michigan Avenue, 17th Floor
> Chicago, IL 60601
> > Phone: 1-800-272-3900
> > > or 1-312-335-8700
> > Website: www.alz.org

National Mental Health Association

> 2001 N. Beauregard Street, 12th Floor
> Alexandria, VA 22311

For suicide crisis: 1-800-SUICIDE (784-2433)

Other calls: 1-800-969-NMHA (6642)

Website: www.nmha.org

MULTIPLE SCLEROSIS
National Multiple Sclerosis Society

733 Third Avenue

New York, NY 10017

Phone: 1-800-FIGHT-MS (344-4867)

Website: www.nmss.org

OSTEOPOROSIS
National Osteoporosis Foundation

1232 22nd Street NW

Washington, DC 20037

Phone: 1-202-223-2226

Website: www.nof.org

PARKINSON'S DISEASE

The following organizations offer pamphlets for patients with Parkinson's Disease and their families.

American Parkinson Disease Association, Inc.

135 Parkinson Avenue

Staten Island, NY 10305

Phone: 1-800-223-2732

Website: www.apdaparkinson.org

National Parkinson Foundation, Inc.

1501 NW 9th Avenue / Bob Hope Road

Miami, FL 33136

Phone: 1-800-327-4545

Website: www.parkinson.org

SPORTS

National Senior Golf Association (NSGA)

     3673 Nottingham Way

     Hamilton Square, NJ 08690

          Phone: 1-800-282-6772

          Website: www.nsgatour.com

The NSGA offers recreational and competitive sports (including golf and tennis) events and trips; discounts on sports equipment, apparel, publications, and leisure products; and Gold Card membership. They have a monthly newsletter, a name-and-address list of members to visit when traveling, and information on where you can play your sport at international resorts overseas.

Over the Hill Gang, International

     1820 West Colorado Avenue

     Colorado Springs, CO 80904

          Phone: 1-719-389-0022

          Website: www.othgi.com

This group offers sports, travel, and adventures at a discount for people age fifty and over (spouses of any age). Over six thousand members make up "gangs" in various cities. They enjoy ballooning, camping, canoeing, fishing, biking, scuba diving, ski trips, surfing, and more. Call, write, or visit their website for information.

U.S. Coast Guard

(boating safety)

     Consumer Information Line

          Phone: 1-800-368-5647

          Website: www.uscgboating.org

The U.S. Coast Guard offers information about boating safety classes, radio licenses, and navigation rules.

STROKE

National Institute of Neurological Disorders and Stroke (NINDS)

NIH Neurological Institute
P.O. Box 5801
Bethesda, MD 20824
Phone: 1-800-352-9424 (voice)
or 1-301-468-5981 (TTY)
Website: www.ninds.nih.gov

This institute offers information on prevention of nervous system disorders and stroke. For information on treatment or rehabilitation services, you might also call a university teaching hospital in your area.

National Stroke Association

9707 East Easter Lane
Englewood, CO 80112
Phone: 1-800-STROKES (787-6537)
Website: www.stroke.org

APPENDIX H

. . . .

ADDITIONAL READING SUGGESTIONS

In addition to the following suggestions, don't miss pages 236–238, where we provide additional reading, catalogs, and websites related to travel, hiking, and so on.

Alter Your Life: Overbooked? Overworked? Overwhelmed? by Dr. Kathleen Hall (Oak Haven)

Are Your Parents Driving You Crazy? Getting to Yes with Competent Aging Parents, Second Edition by Joseph A. Ilardo, Ph.D., L.C.S.W. and Carole R. Rothman, Ph.D. (VanderWyk & Burnham)

Are You Smart, or What? A Bizarre Book of Games & Fun for Everyone by Pasqual J. Battaglia (International Puzzle Features)

AstroFit: The Astronaut Program for Anti-Aging by William J. Evans, Ph.D. and Gerald Secor Couzens (The Free Press/Simon & Schuster)

Awakening at Midlife: A Guide to Reviving Your Spirit, Recreating Your Life, and Returning to Your Truest Life by Kathleen A. Brehony (Riverhead Books/Penguin Group)

Caring for Yourself While Caring for Your Aging Parents: How to Help, How to Survive, Third Edition by Claire Berman (Owl Books/Henry Holt)

Chicken Soup for the Caregiver's Soul: Stories to Inspire Caregivers in the Home, the Community and the World by Jack Canfield, Mark Victor Hansen, LeAnn Thieman, L.P.N. (Health Communications Inc.)

Cooking for Children: No Mess, No Fuss, No Problem by Dagmar von Cramm and Michael Brauner (Silverback Books)

Creative Visualization: Use the Power of Your Imagination to Create What You Want in Your Life, 25th Anniversary Edition by Shakti Gawain (New World Library)

Eldercare 911: The Caregiver's Complete Handbook for Making Decisions by Susan Beerman, M.S., M.S.W. and Judith Rappaport-Musson, C.S.A. (Prometheus Books)

The Fearless Caregiver: How to Get the Best Care for Your Loved One and Still Have a Life of Your Own by Gary Barg (Capital Books)

Feel Nifty After 50! Top Tips to Help Women Grow Young, Second Edition by Jo Peddicord (Golden Aspen Publishing)

Get Organized, Get Published! 225 Ways to Make Time for Success by Don Aslett and Carol Cartaino (Writer's Digest Books/F&W Publications)

The Glory Walk, A Memoir about Alzheimer's by Cathryn E. Smith (VanderWyk & Burnham)

The Grandparent Guide: The Definitive Guide to Coping with the Challenges of Modern Grandparenting by Arthur Kornhaber, M.D. (Contemporary Books/McGraw-Hill)

***Handbook to a Happier Life: A Simple Guide to Creating the
Life You've Always Wanted*** by Jim Donovan (New World Library)

How to Create the Life You Want After 50 by Sara Brown, Ph.D.
(Savvy Sisters Press)

***The New Retirement: The Ultimate Guide to the Rest of Your
Life*** by Jan Cullinane, Cathy Fitzgerald (Rodale Books)

***Organizing from the Inside Out: The Foolproof System for
Organizing Your Home, Your Office, and Your Life, Second
Edition*** by Julie Morgenstern (Owl Books/Henry Holt)

***Profit from Your Vacation Home Dream: The Complete Guide to
a Savvy Financial and Emotional Investment*** by Christine
Karpinski (Kaplan Publishing)

***Qi Energy for Health and Healing: A Comprehensive Guide to
Accessing Your Healing Energy*** by Mallory Fromm, Ph.D.
(Avery/Penguin Putnam)

***Retire and Thrive: Remarkable People, Age 50-plus, Share Their
Creative, Productive, and Profitable Retirement Strategies*** by
Robert K. Otterbourg (Kiplinger Books)

***Retirement on a Shoestring: Maximizing Your Options, Income,
and Enjoyment for the Golden Years, Fifth Edition*** (Choose
Retirement Series) by John Howells (Globe Pequot)

***Save Your Face: The Truth about Facial Aging, Its Prevention
and "Cure"*** by Brooke Rutledge Seckel, M.D. (Peach Publications)

***Sisters and Brothers All These Years: Taking Another Look at the
Longest Relationship in Your Life*** by Lillian S. Hawthorne
(VanderWyk & Burnham)

· ·

Spiritual Passages: Embracing Life's Sacred Journey by Drew Leder, M.D., Ph.D. (Tarcher/Putnam)

Twenty-Two Prayer Poems for Care Givers: Inspired by A Course in Miracles® and Other Sacred Teachings by Donna Iona Drozda (Wren House)

Volunteering: 101 Ways You Can Improve the World and Your Life by Douglas M. Lawson (Alti Publishers)

What Are Old People For? How Elders Will Save the World by William H. Thomas, M.D. (VanderWyk & Burnham)

Worry-Free Retirement Living: Choosing a Full-Service Retirement Community by Loni Smith and Ralph Smith (Publish America)

YOU: The Owner's Manual: An Insider's Guide to the Body That Will Make You Healthier and Younger by Michael F. Roizen and Mehmet C. Oz (Collins)

APPENDIX I

REAL-LIFE RETIREMENTS

It is truly exciting when we get feedback from readers. Here are some examples of notes about real-life retirement experiences we've received.

• One woman advises making careful plans about where you will live regarding mobility, expense, transportation, and being close to relatives. Choose only activities you really enjoy. Use the library for books, computers, videos, DVDs, newspapers, and magazines.

• One couple likes to read, quilt, knit, work at a food pantry, track ancestry, buy and sell on eBay, attend theater and concerts. They plan to travel, and also to volunteer at a law school to be clients in mock legal trials or to sit in on interesting court sessions.

• One couple loves to travel and plans to spend two weeks in Texas working for Habitat for Humanity.

• One couple worked so well together they were the oldest couple ever to make the Final Four in the "Amazing Race" TV show. They like to bike, kayak, golf, travel, and dance. He also teaches a course at a community college, and she volunteers at hospice.

• Another couple sold their home and possessions and for two years traveled to visit family and friends—and while there, they did projects for their hosts. They later bought a condo in and moved to Hawaii where they now paddle six-person and one- and two-person outrigger canoes and do yoga. They also volunteer at the Olympics and the Hawaii Ironman Triathlon World Championships. They advise you to step out of your old life and be truly open to new things and possibly a different part of the country/world.

One theme runs throughout: being able to do what you want, when you want, where you want. It is the greatest pleasure in retirement. Please think about sharing your story of retirement with us; you could be a source of encouragement and inspiration to other retirees if the idea to expand this section in future editions becomes a reality.

INDEX

A

AARP, 16–17, 60
Abacus, 115
Abalone, 115
Abroad, 115
Abstract, 115
Abuse, 40, 115
Accordion, 115
Acrobatics, 115
Active, 115
Acupuncture, 30, 75, 81, 116
Addict, 116
Adopt a highway, 15
Adopt a Native-Elder, 15
Adoption open records, 15
Aerobics, 116
Afghan, 116
Africa, 116
Aging, 16–17, 65, 239
Aging family members, 16
Aging Network Services, 239
Airlines, 216–217
Airplane, 16, 116
Albums, photo, 78
Alcatraz, 68
Alcohol and drugs, 16
Alcoholism, 116
Allergies, 239

Alternative medicine, 75
Alzheimer's disease, 16, 245
Amaryllis, 116
America, 116
American Academy of Otolaryngology, 244
American Association of Retired Persons. *See* AARP
American Cancer Society, 240
American Diabetes Association, 241
American Heart Association, 244–245
American Lung Association, 245
American Parkinson Disease Association, 246
American Printing House for the Blind, 242–243
American Sign Language, 92
American Speech-Language-Hearing Association, 242

Amputee, 117
Amuse, 117
Animal, 117
Animation/computer skills, 17
Antarctic, 117
Antares, 117
Antique collecting, 33
Aphid, 117
Aquariums, 17
Arbor Day, 243
Archaeology, 18, 212
Archery, 18
Arm Activation, 195
Art, 18, 44, 178
Art Car Weekend, 18
Art gallery on wheels, 18
Arthritis Foundation, 240
Artifacts, 18–19
Artist, 19, 117
Arts and crafts worldwide, 19
Astronomers, 19–20
Auction, 117
Audience, 117
Audubon, 243
Australia, 118
Authors, 20. *See also* Write
Autobiography, 20, 107